Art of Seduction

How to Talk to Anyone. Learn how to Seduce People with your Voice and Body Language, through new Manipulation Techniques |Love-Work-Self Confidence| 3Books in1

by

Ellen Lewis

First paperback Edition January 2023

Book by:

Ellen Lewis

For More Info:

ellen.lewis@gmail.com

Table of Contents

Introduction

What you say is truly important, but how you say it also matters. Being aware of your body language while communicating with others helps you convey your true feelings more and reach an understanding to a whole new level.

Understanding the situation relies heavily on communication. However, it is not just limited to words. According to the Albert Mehrabian Communication Model, communication is only 7% verbal, while 38% vocal and 55% visual. It means that 93% of communication is non-verbal in nature. Thus, mastering the non-verbal aspect of communication is a must.

Body language is simply the unspoken element of communication that we use or project to reveal our true feelings and emotions. It can be as simple as a relaxed facial expression; the mouth upturned and eyes wrinkled, that breaks out into a real smile; a head tilt indicates that you are listening; sitting or standing upright to express interest or using hand motions directing focus and attention.

If you want to improve your communication skills, you need to learn how to read people. In any scenario, body language will work for or against you. But once you know other people's body language, the effects can be astounding.

There are several ways that body language can be helpful. For instance, it can help you read a person's reactions and intentions with more clarity and accuracy. It can also help you understand the emotions behind someone's words. Understanding how people react and what they are thinking makes it easier to connect with them and form meaningful relationships.

You can boost your confidence through body language. You'll communicate more easily with others when you know how to read body language cues. It can help you ace a client meeting or a job interview and make for a better career.

Body language will also help you improve your dating life. You'll be able to

1

figure out if a girl likes you and make a better first impression on her when you know how to read body language. It will develop your confidence level in various social settings.

As body language can help you communicate your genuine thoughts and feelings, it can also help you understand others. For example, if a person's arms are drawn close to their body and hunched over a little, it could mean they feel threatened or that they feel cornered by something or someone. If the eyes are roaming around the room, it could be because they are feeling paranoid and not sure where to focus. It is essential to know how these cues are displayed because they can reveal a lot about the person.

Learning how to communicate using body language is something that most people struggle to do well. If you want to discover more and be an expert at it, this book is going to help you out. You will learn how reading body language is part of a more extensive skill set that includes treating people kindly and getting what you want from them.

PART I.

How the Body Talks

Understanding Body Language

Interpersonal interactions have been profoundly impacted by body language. And simple hand gestures can be understood in a variety of ways. A hand gesture can be changed by other body movements and facial expressions, which can further confuse issues. Additionally, it might not be as obvious as body language.

People still don't realize it, but their body gestures are a sign of unwelcome behaviors that can spread to others. You need to be mindful of your movements since the behaviors you exhibit can be used to judge you on a number of occasions because different personality types exhibit different behaviors.

It's important to keep in mind that these outward expressions of our bodies can reveal information about us as well as others, in addition to the motions we refer to as body language. Since our body language and attitude are both often indicative of how we are feeling, it has been said that the body is a mirror to the soul. Actually, they are going to tell us what emotions we feel.

Nonverbal communication is a fascinating byproduct of our physiology, environment, and society. We might be able to inform others about our attitudes. Depending on the relationships we are in, we may inherit particular traits that influence how we present ourselves to others and how we employ various non-verbal communication techniques. You might conduct yourself differently around work colleagues compared to family members. Perhaps because your comfort zone shifts, you are more watchful in different situations, which affects how you react.

You don't physically display yourself to others. Many of the body's responses appear to be more unconscious in nature, where we communicate with others, even though other movements are intentional. Unfortunately, implicit body language frequently reveals facts about ourselves that we do not want other people to know. There are various bodily cues that can give us suggestions or feelings about how we're feeling emotionally.

We watch others' body language and interpret it, especially while they are speaking. Hand and facial gestures are used throughout the conversation. If we were not aware of this, another person's words might not have the same effect.

One way to more effectively perceive other signals is to become more self-aware. Heed expressions and emotions. Consider how your words and nonverbal cues can work together to express a feeling. You can better comprehend your relationships with people if you learn to read your own body language.

The best illustration of unconscious body language is in children. Even after learning words, young toddlers occasionally convey their emotions nonverbally. Typically, you can tell whether a child is unhappy or frustrated. Preschoolers and toddlers frequently communicate vocally. Similarly, young children and babies are quite adept at reading our body language.

It's interesting to consider that the movements that young toddlers use to communicate their needs eventually aid brain development and prepare them for later spoken communication. Children focus on an adult's face when they are being spoken to right away. How did they come to know that? The underlying explanation is genetics, thus perhaps eyes are windows to the soul!

What Is Body Language

Interaction is a skill among humans. It may take place in discrete and simple ways. We both talk and write. But we can also communicate without speaking. This non-verbal communication speaks to our relationships in the same way that words do when communicating ideas. Possibly more significant than conveying the message. We're having a meta-conversation about contact!

If speaking to an individual, or if words simply aren't cutting it, we also need to be explicit about how to understand the content of our message. The manner in which we do this reveals something about our relationship with them, or at the very least, how we view them. Sounds are unable to accomplish that. Thinking about our feelings is preferable to showing them. Our bodies convey the significance of our words. This language is utilized for nonverbal communication in the Saussurian culture. We don't even care to use it frequently. When we touch our partner during a conversation, it conveys a completely different meaning than when we don't. It is simply not possible to communicate without employing non-verbal cues; writing is the only exception.

Body language is a nonverbal form of communication in which the gestures, attitudes, and postures of the body "talk."

Body language was used long before vocal communication, and it continues to be one of the most fundamental means of communication for people. According to experts, nonverbal communication makes up about 93% of all human communication. Without using words, 55% of communication consists of body language such as postures, gestures, and facial emotions. Loudness and vocalization, which includes voice tone, rhythm, and speed, are also crucial and account for 38% of messages sent.

Different emotions can be expressed through the arms, legs, head, and facial expression. A person might not be interested in the conversation or the other person if, for instance, they do not keep eye contact when the other person is speaking to them. On the other hand, a person's crossed arms can be interpreted as defensive and indicative of insecurity. According to social psychologist Amy Cuddy, our posture not only affects how others perceive us but also how we see ourselves. In addition, Cuddy distinguishes between powerful and non-powerful attitudes, depending on how they affect our sense of self. A good posture can be helpful in a variety of situations, such as job interviews.

Importance of Body Language

Humans can always communicate because even without using words, they can convey meaning to others by their physical presence, their physical attributes, their facial characteristics, their attire, and their posture. Since an image has a lot of power and a person may learn a lot about another by using their sense of sight, body language still has a greater impact on the recipient than words do.

A person's skill to make gestures can be seen in their body language. It should be emphasized that among the various body parts, the face has a remarkable ability for expression due to the strength of the glance and the smile. Controlling your body language allows you to be more mindful of the message you send in daily scenarios like a work interview, a first love date, or a couple's conversation.

You provide a confusing message to the recipient if what you physically convey conflicts with what you verbally state. For instance, even if a candidate has a strong CV, he may still come across as uninterested in the position if he dresses sloppily and arrives late for the interview. To improve communication, one must pay close attention to the details.

Despite the fact that there have been several studies on body language, it is important to realize that it is not possible to scientifically interpret what each gesture signifies. A yawn, for instance, may indicate boredom. However, it can also mean feeling hungry or that the person is sleepy because they have not slept all night. Putting things in context is essential to avoid making hasty deductions from certain gestures. To know a person is a long process that requires time and many hours of conversation.

The body language shows the reality of the human being composed of body and mind. While you transmit your ideas through your word, the body expresses its discomfort or well-being through bodily presence.

If you want to learn to have a better command of the communication of your own body, then I encourage you to participate in a public speaking course where you will get enough information. You can see the importance of body language by doing the exercise of watching a movie on TV without volume. You will notice how you capture information from what you observe.

Our communication consists of verbal and non-verbal, in which we communicate non-verbally up to 93 percent of the time. The tone of voice, stance, hand motions, facial expressions, all this and more are our non-verbal communication.

Our vocabulary learns to talk, builds it in school, but our body's language is not taught. That's something we're doing alone. The way we stand to look at others means something. How well we can use them becomes essential.

When we meet new people, our body language changes. When we meet our schoolteacher, for instance, we stand straight, don't flinch, and are friendly; but, when we meet our friends, we switch up the manner by going up to them, shaking their hand or hugging them, and relaxing. We are more drawn to people who have a positive outlook and a welcoming grin.

The ability to communicate what we are thinking is a key component of body language. We may learn about someone's feelings through their body language. For instance, a person might tell their supervisor that they are glad to consider

7

this, but their body language may indicate that they are not really. This will assist a boss in selecting the right candidate for this position. This might be a crucial hype.If she doesn't have a conscience, she can do an acceptable role if another employee will make a life-long client of this small work.

The deciding factor in a work interview may be body language. When the body language of the candidate shows that he is easy to manage and trust, he is more likely to get the job, particularly in this challenging job market. We addressed the fact earlier that particular body language is considered awkward and unregulated. These are some of the same characteristics which make a worker less confident and relaxed.

Through friendship, the language of one's body may show that someone cares about what the other person says or not. Leaning into the conversation indicates that he is interested in listening to what the other person says. Leaning back will suggest that he was unselfish or thought superior. Sitting up and standing near during speech may mean that someone actively attempts to convince or control the discussion. Hearing someone when you don't have eye contact means you aren't alert, just waiting for the chance to speak. It gives your friend the impression that you just don't know what they say, and that they cannot listen carefully when it's your turn to chat.

Reading Body Language

As you would expect, this element of communication skills is important in human relationships, both in the workplace and in private life. In particular, it assumes a relevant part of the relationship between man and woman. The language of the female body is different from the language of the male body. Remember that to better carry out the interpretation of body language, help can come from proxemics, a discipline that precisely studies distances within proximity relationships. Would you ever have thought that flirting could be the subject of a scientific discipline? It probably gave you the importance of communication and why it is well studied in every corner of the world.

When it comes to non-verbal communication, the first thing to say is that it is challenging to decipher because body language is not an exact science. However, in a reasonably sure way, some signals are associated with a precise meaning. Scholars usually group body language signals into groups and subgroups that refer to the body's parts for convenience. To which they belong, we, too, in our practical guide to body language, will resort to this type of subdivision.

We will analyze the body parts: eyes, mouth, head, arms, hands, handshakes, legs and feet, personal space. If you are moving your head quickly, you are probably quite impatient to know how to read body language, and so here we go.

Eyes

The eyes have enormous importance in our body language: just think that the human being can make eye contact with another human being even 90 to 120 feet away. There is also a close association between the eyes and the brain:

looking to the right is typical of someone who is in a creative phase while looking to the left usually has to do with memory.

Here is a possible reading of some signals that we send to others (or that others send to us) through the eyes:

- Looking to the right indicates creating, manufacturing with the imagination (also in the sense of lying); if below, it can mean that the person is drawing from his inner sensations or that he has feelings.

- Looking left means using memory, remembering, recovering facts; if upwards, they indicate security and certainty.

- Direct eye contact when speaking indicates honesty, but it can also be flaunted by liars who know they are lying; while listening, on the other hand, shows interest, attention, sometimes physical attraction.

- The widening of the eyes is also a sign of interest in a sexual nature.

- Rubbing your eyes or an eye indicates amazement, disbelief, disturbance, in some cases boredom or need to sleep.

- Rolling one's eyes can mean resignation and frustration.

- Dilating the pupils may in some cases indicate excitement or desire.

- Blinking can indicate excitement or agitation; if the eyes are fixed, this can mean a concentration or, when turned towards someone, hostility.

- Raising the eyebrows (or just one eyebrow) corresponds to a friendly greeting when the action is short-lived (flash eyebrow); if the eyebrows remain raised longer, this indicates surprise, fear, perplexity.

- Last but not least, winking indicates complicity.

Mouth

The mouth is associated with many body language cues, whether or not there is verbal communication. Smiling is undoubtedly one of the first signs of openness to others, but there are many types of smiles, some of which may also indicate rejection.

Let's find out the meaning of various signals associated with this part of our body:

- Smiling only with the mouth indicates a false, not sincere smile.

- Smiling through gritted teeth means rejection, dislike, or distrust.

- Smiling asymmetrically, with only one part of the face, indicates sarcasm or contrast.

- Protruding the lower lip indicates that you are irritated or moved (about to cry).

- Laughing with your mouth open indicates, accompanying the laughter with body movements, that we feel comfortable.

- Biting one's lips indicates nervousness or tension (in some cases, however, nibbling one's lips can also be a sexual invitation).

- Teeth grinding indicates worry, anxiety, fear.

- Chewing a pen or pencil has a self-reassuring function like sucking your thumb and in some cases smoking a cigarette.

- Putting the tongue in the center of the mouth indicates refusal. It is, in fact, the gesture we make when we put something we don't like in our mouth.

- Closing one's mouth with one or two hands is an unconscious gesture of self-regulation that indicates shock, amazement, sometimes embarrassment, as it is as if we wanted to block words so as not to express something wrong.

- Nail-biting is the result of a situation of stress, anxiety, and frustration. For some, it represents a form of aggression towards oneself.

Head

The head tends to determine the body's general direction, but it is also a very vulnerable part as it contains the brain. Since it rests on a very flexible structure (the neck), the head can move practically in all directions, and all these movements are associated with these meanings of body language:

- Nodding your head means that you have agreed with our interlocutor,

11

but if you do it too slowly, it could be a sign of falsehood, too fast of impatience.

- Raising the head upwards indicates pride, arrogance but, in some cases, also courage, vigilance.

- Tilting the head to one side indicates submission, the exposure of the neck is a sign of confidence.

- Leaning your head forward communicates interest, positivity. If instead it is downward, it can indicate reproach or disapproval.

- Shaking your head, especially if vigorously, indicates disagreement.

- Bowing your head on your chest indicates shame, abandonment, and defeat.

Arms

The arms are relatively reliable indicators of a person's mood: clenching the components, for example, indicates defense while opening the elements, keeping the palms open in front of you communicates safety and openness. We see other signs that you can communicate through the body language associated with the arms, also in combination with other parts of the body:

- Crossing arms and legs is a sign of defense if the fists are also closed with hostility.

- Girding one arm with the other, a typical gesture of women, indicates nervousness or self-protection.

- Bringing your arms behind your back with folded hands, typical of men, indicates strength, authority and self-confidence.

- Placing an arm table with an object on the opposite side can indicate nervousness, also scratching an arm or shoulder with the opposite hand.

- To hold the arm in front of the body, especially with the hand close to the genitals, indicates defense, self-protection (it is typical of women who hold the shoulder bag on the front as if they want to create an additional barrier).

Language of Hands

The body language that involves the hands is extensive. They tend to interact with many other parts of the body; also, the manual gestures only partially respond to voluntary action. Most of the time, they are involuntary movements, such as touching the nose. Examples of prearranged signals are to do the OK with the thumb up or to greet; sometimes, we also use our hands voluntarily to communicate, for example, the size of an object. Here are the possible interpretations of some signals with the hands:

- Raising your open palm upwards is a sign of submission, honesty, and peace given "that you have no weapon in your hand."

- Hands raising on your face with open fingers is a defensive, sometimes offensive, position, and also returning the hands.

- Placing your hand on your heart indicates sincerity, the will to be believed.

- Pointing the finger at a person is a sign of threat, aggression; if the finger is pointed upwards, it is typical of a person who wants to add emphasis to what he is saying.

- Moving the index from one side to the other communicates refusal.

- Resting the fingertips of one hand on those of the other hand forming a triangle is typical of someone who is reflecting or explaining something complex; moving your fingertips on each other as if imitating a spider on a mirror increases concentration and reflection.

- Moving the palms of the hands facing downward up and down corresponds to the urge to keep calm (a gesture often used by teachers to observe a class at bay.

- Rubbing your hands together indicates a positive expectation, savoring a win or a pleasant result in advance.

- Touching or scratching your nose with your hands while speaking indicates lying or exaggerating information content.

- Covering one's ears with one's hands is a gesture of refusal, instead of pulling one's earlobe indicating indecision.

- Caressing your chin with your hands, a rare gesture in women but frequent in men, indicates that you are thinking about something; if the hand supports the chin, it means that you are pondering what to do about something, but if the action is prolonged it can also indicate tiredness, boredom.

- Scratching the neck usually indicates doubt, disbelief.

- Squeezing the wrist with one hand can indicate anxiety, worry, especially if the wrist is rotated inside the needle several times.

- Putting your hands in your pockets indicates disinterest, boredom, refusal to take action.

Handshakes

Once reserved only for men but now also extended to women, a handshake's firmness is not a reliable indicator of firmness of character, but many believe it is. However, the handshake can say many things about us and our relationship with others:

- Handshake with the palm down indicates dominance, willingness to take over.

- Handshake with the palm upwards communicates openness, hospitality.

- A two-handed handshake, in some cases, indicates honesty, reliability, affection. In others, paternalism or attempt to control the person in front of you (even when the second encircles the opposite arm).

- A vigorous handshake indicates enthusiasm, vigor, attempt to transfer energy to others.

- A weak handshake is not necessarily related to a submissive character. It often depends on other factors such as mood, gender membership, age, profession (musicians or surgeons may have delicate handshakes because the hands are their work tool, therefore, to be treated with caution).

- Also, avoid associating a firm handshake with a strong character. It could instead be an attempt to mask one's weakness or wrong intentions, such as the will to hide or do harm.

Legs and Feet

Legs and feet can provide useful clues about feelings and moods, as long as you can decipher the signs.

However, always keep in mind that the position of the legs also affects gender (males usually tend to keep the legs more open than women), education, and age (the elderly both for joint problems and for education tend to keep narrower legs when seated only):

- Sitting with crossed legs indicates prudence, confidentiality (in some cases if you also show disinterest), availability, openness.

- Parallel legs with knees well closed when seated are a typical female attitude indicating good manners or fear.

- Pointing the knees towards someone with crossed legs indicates interest in that person.

- Closing the cross legs keeping the legs independent is a security posture that denotes an open, unconventional character; if, on the other hand, the legs are surrounded by the arms, the position indicates self-protection.

- Open legs when seated (especially in males) indicate arrogance, self-confidence, in some cases generalized sexual interest (the knees not only pointed towards a single subject but towards a wider audience).

- Legs entwined while seated (in the female) may indicate sexual interest as the inner part of the thigh is exposed, or insecurity, search for protection (especially if with the hands placed on the inside).

- Clenching your knees with your hands while sitting with your legs parallel indicates a defensive attitude or that you are uncomfortable.

Body Language Analysis

You may be wondering why it is appropriate to learn other people's body language. It may be a challenge, but it is important that you are aware. The ability to understand other people's body language saves you a lot of time that you would have probably been researching why they did something.

To acquire the art of understanding people's non-verbal communication is a hard thing. You may be wondering how you can focus on learning other people's cues while you do not even know yourself fully. Well, this book would help you demystify the art of understanding body language for different people.

All of us are subconscious experts in interpreting the thoughts of other individuals around us. In the woolly mammoth age, we developed these abilities since our life depended on them, and the unconscious mind would work more efficiently than the conscious mind. However, when we make this unconscious understanding conscious, it does not yield a good result. Practically, we can respond with lightning speed to dodge a fist that some whiny brat throws in our way, or to jump out from the way of an approaching car before we can think about it explicitly.

Stuff we don't say will in any case relay quantities of information, from our outward appearance to our body movements. It was evident right away that visual correspondence could account for 60 to 65 percent of all correspondence. Understanding the visual correspondence is important, but other considerations, such as the setting, must also be considered. If there is no functional experience in an operation, the party should be investigated in certain situations.

The implicit part of communication is nonverbal contact. For example, our signals, outward appearances and posture. When we are able to "interpret" these signals, we can, for example, use them to our advantage. It will motivate you to understand the full meaning of what someone is saying and to improve our understanding of people's reactions to what we say and do.

We can also use it to guide our visual correspondence, making us seem more optimistic, sharing, and friendly in general.

When it comes to personal and professional success, being able to communicate effectively is important, but it's not just the words you say that tell the tale. It's all down to your body language. Your best communication techniques are movements, stance, eye contact, facial expressions and tone of voice. These have the power to perplex, weaken, offend, create confidence, attract others, or relax someone.

Many times, what someone says and what their body language suggest are diametrically opposed. Nonverbal contact has the ability to achieve five goals:

- Substitute—Instead of a verbal message, it could be used.

- Accent—It can emphasize or underline your verbal message.

- Supplement—It could add to or complement what you're saying verbally.

- Repetition—It has the ability to reinforce and repeat the verbal message.

- Contradict—It might make your audience believe you're misleading by going against what you're trying to tell verbally.

Nonverbal Communication Signs That Are Popular

The following are some helpful tips for learning how to read nonverbal interactions and better understanding the people you interact with.

Focus on the Face

Even if people are conscious of their physical appearance, if you pay attention, you will notice important nonverbal signs. When attempting to decipher nonverbal actions, pay close attention to the mouth. A smile that matches a facial expression is a positive sign. Smiling is an important nonverbal cue to keep an eye on. There are many styles of smiles, including real smiles and smiles that are influenced. A genuine smile encompasses the entire face, while a fake smile focuses solely on the lips. A genuine smile indicates that the individual is upbeat and positive about the people around them.

Covering your mouth or covering your lips with your hands or fingertips while speaking is another indication that you're lying.

Look at the Eyes

Concentrate on who the person in question looks or appears when human action is directed toward them. Making direct eye-to-eye contact can demonstrate boredom, impartiality, or being deceptive—especially if someone is out of your field of vision. On the other hand, if the person is in front of you, he or she might display anxiety or agreement. Often, look at the students to see if everyone is responding favorably to you. Mental exertion may cause pupils to dilate. If someone is focused on someone or something they like, their pupils will dilate in this way. Pupils can be difficult to observe, but under the right circumstances, you should be able to recognize them. The rate at which a person squints may reveal a lot about what's going on inside. When people think too hard or are pulled, their squinting rate increases. An increased blinking rate can often mean that someone is lying, and looking closely can help you find out. If someone, for example, looks at the door often, this might indicate that they need to leave. Looking at someone can indicate a desire to speak with them. Eye contact, as well as looking up and to the right, may mean that the person is lying, while looking up and to one side may indicate that the person is telling the truth. The theory may be that when people look to the right, their imaginative mind thinks up a story, and when they look up and to the left, they are remembering a true memory.

Look for Head Movements

When people speak to you, the speed at which they turn their heads indicates their understanding—or lack thereof. Slow hanging indicates that they are engrossed in what you're saying and would like you to continue speaking. Fast hanging indicates that they have comprehended enough and that you must either finish speaking or give them a chance to answer. Tilting your head sideways while speaking will demonstrate your interest in the subject. Tilting back may be a sign of weakness or vulnerability.

Take a Look at the Other Person's Feet

The feet are a part of the body that often "releases" fundamental nonverbal signals. The explanation for this is that people send nonverbal messages with their feet, but they are more concerned with their outer appearances and upper body than with what their feet show.

Proximity is Also a Factor

Allow others to stand or sit beside you to see if they have a good impression of you. One of the best indicators of affinity is standing or sitting next to another. If, on the other hand, someone backs up or steps away from you as you get closer, this could mean that you aren't really that close.

To see if the other person is reflecting on you, conduct a test.

Reflecting entails imitating the visual correspondence of another person. When you're in front of someone, see if they behave in the same way you do. If you're sitting at a table with someone and you put your elbow on the table, wait up to ten seconds to see if they do the same.

Taking a sip of a beverage at the same time is another typical reflective behavior. If anyone imitates your visual correspondence, it's a good indicator that they're attempting to form a bond with you. Start shifting the body to see if the other person responds in the same way.

Focus on the Hands

Hands, like feet, have multiple nonverbal cues. These are important suggestions. When the individual is up, check and see if they have their hands in their pockets. Look for simple hand gestures, such as when the person you're communicating with puts their hands in their pockets or puts their hands on their heads. This may indicate everything from fear to deception. Hand movements can convey a lot of details. Individuals can talk a lot with their hands (this nonverbal cue should be looked at at meetings). An elbow on the table indicates that the individual is paying attention and tuning in. When someone puts something between you and them, it may be a boundary that is supposed to keep the other person out. For instance, if two individuals are speaking and one is holding a stack of papers in front of the other, this may be a sign of nonverbal communication.

Lower Body

Arms transmit a lot of data. When an individual shifts his weight from one leg to the other, body language experts have found that this is a signal of discomfort. It is common for individuals who are nervous or uncomfortable to shift their weight between their feet when standing or sitting.

The arms and hands are another major body area that communicate non-verbal cues. The individual's arms will often cross across his chest in a defensive posture when he feels threatened by someone else. The fingers of both hands might be interlocked. As the individual becomes increasingly nervous or frustrated, his arms begin to move from their defensive position and are placed in front of his body along with his hands. The palms of the hands might be placed on the surface in front of him. This is a sign that the individual feels threatened in some way, and he is now ready to move forward should the threat become more threatening.

Legs will show whether or not a person is accessible and at ease. They may also be displaying their influence or showing where they want to go.

Legs Touching

Only a person's bottom or thighs would be able to be touched when standing. This can be done seductively or by slapping their legs together as if to suggest, "Let's go." It may also be a representation of frustration. This is when you must pay attention to the conversation's meaning. This is a critical point.

Look at the Arms

The doors to the body and, by definition, to yourself, are the weapons. When someone folds their arms while speaking with you, it could be interpreted as a guarded, blocking signal. Nervousness, vulnerability, or a closed personality may all be exhibited through crossed arms. If crossed arms are go with by a sincere smile and a generally loosened up posture, it could mean that all is assured, loosened up. When an individual position their hands on their hips, they are searching for power, and men are more likely to do so than women.

Pointing Feet

Look at a person's feet to see where their attention is focused. Their feet will often point in the direction of what they are thinking about or focusing on. Each individual has a lead foot, which is decided by their dominant hand. Your lead foot will be pointing toward them if you're interested in what they're doing. If you want to ignore them, though, you'll find your foot pointed in the direction of an exit or the direction you want to go. Look where a person's feet are pointing while they are seated during the discussion to see what they are really interested in.

Confidence In People

People who want to appear larger normally sit with their legs splayed open and lean back. They could even stretch their arms out in front of their heads and lock them behind their backs. People that are dominant, superior, or confident, usually use this.

Shyness in People

Women are more likely than men to engage in this conduct. Anyone who is shy or uneasy can entangle their legs by crossing them over and over in an effort to block out negative emotions and make them seem smaller. When people are standing, they will do another shy leg twirl roll. As if scratching an itch, cross one leg over the other and hook the other foot behind the knee.

It's all in the Eyes—Clues to

Revealing True Intentions

Our eyes are the windows to our souls. They provide a wealth of information, but what is it really telling us? Humans have been reading others' eyes for thousands of years. We read other's eyes to detect deception. This has been done to keep our own offspring safe from harm, protect our community, or even achieve some revenge. Even if you aren't in the business of observing the world around you—reading people's facial expressions and eye contact is still an important skill that everyone should possess.

You can effortlessly spot a liar when they tell one. The struggle is, most individuals do not realize that they are telling a lie. They're not aware of the small, but important details that give away their intentions. This is the reason why there are so many myths surrounding what to look for in people's eyes to discern if what they say is the truth or false. We are going to go through some of these myths and discuss them; then we will discuss some of the facts and history surrounding eye contact and lying.

Eye movement is key when trying to determine if someone is lying or telling the truth. According to Dr. Lillian Glass, a body language and behavioral expert, a person's eyes will dart around the room when they are spinning a tale to make you believe their story. The problem with this is although the eyes may look like they are dashing everywhere, if you closely observe what their eyes are actually focused on, there is way more communication going on than just darting back and forth. So while one might think that looking for eye movements while someone is telling a lie can be useful you need to look more closely at what those eyes are looking at.

One of the most measurable points when children are tested for neurological challenges is their ability to maintain good eye contact. The willingness to lock eyes with someone else during a conversation, though a minor detail, speaks volumes about the child's level of function. A child is considered high on the social spectrum if they can maintain direct eye contact during their tests. Incapability to preserve eye contact, on the other hand, may be a symptom of autism or even social anxiety. The eyes reveal small truths about our biology's inner workings.

Can you think of the initial thing that comes to your awareness as soon as you meet someone? Usually, their eyes show facets of elegance that appeal to first impressions. Many people are remembered for the shape, color and size of their eyes. We are neurologically wired to be visual beings that create connections based on what we see. In certain cases, these relations are labeled by the energy we emit. How do our eyes interact with those receptors, considering that the brain regulates every part of our bodies?

The Brain and the Eye

The retina acts as the eye's gatekeeper. Anything we see passes through the retina and is then passed to two separate parts of the eye: rods, which regulate our night vision, and cones, which control our day-to-day vision tasks including color translation, reading, writing and scanning. Various neurons migrate around the eye, interacting with various functions to bear distinct signals. These signals are then carried into the cerebral cortex through the optic nerve. The cerebral cortex functions similarly to a movie theater in the brain. It is in control of our visual receptors, which are involved in vision, memory and thought. Researchers have found that when our eye sees something pleasurable, the pupil actually expands. This phenomenon demonstrates that we think what we see. We can shape opinions, draw conclusions and even analyze body movements using this method.

Understanding body language requires an understanding of how our eyes interact with our brain and perception. Since we interact with every part of our bodies, it's only normal that the eyes play a significant role in this type of communication. To the untrained eye, the eyes can appear one-dimensional. Their subtle gestures, on the other hand, can reveal everything you need to know about a human.

Eye Contact

Direct eye contact may signify a change in mood. Self-assurance is certainly one of the most important markers of locking eyes. Recruiters will often advise their interviewees to look the interviewer in the eye to show awareness while vetting for a work. This specifies to the interviewer that you are unafraid to take on any mission. Animals use eye contact to assess superiority in the same way humans do. A trainer, for example, will often look a dog he is training in the eyes to demonstrate dominance. The dog can learn to obey the trainer's orders if he locks his eyes and refuses to move. Humans use dominant signs to communicate as well. Fear is defeated by direct eye contact. It demonstrates that you are at ease with the discussion and even shows interest.

Furthermore, everything revolves around the idea of equilibrium. Too much direct eye contact can be daunting to the person receiving it. Others can become uneasy as a result of your intense gaze, and they may even doubt your sanity. Imagine holding a conversation with someone who is continuously poking you in the eyes. And when you averted your attention, their gaze stayed focused on you. Surely, you'd categorize them as incredibly strange. It's always important to be aware of what your eyes are doing, as staring can be considered disrespectful in some cultures.

Dilated Pupils

The pupils send out complex signals that detect even the tiniest changes in the body. People's pupils grow larger when they are asked a tough question, according to studies. According to a 1973 report, when the brain is forced to think beyond its capacities, the pupils narrow. The pupils are also important markers of brain tension. A small spotlight will be shined into the eyes of patients by health care practitioners to ensure that their pupils are natural. The brain is not in pain if the pupils are of equal size and respond to the shining light. Any imbalance, on the other hand, may suggest a severe brain injury.

As previously stated, dilated pupils show intense interest, if not agreement. Your eyes dilate almost instantly when you see or hear something that catches your attention. When an individual is shown a representation of something they agree with, the same thing happens. In 1969, a well-known researcher set out to prove that pupil dilation can disclose political allegiances. The participants' eyes dilated when they were shown images of political figures they admired.

When shown an opposing photo, however, the pupils dilated and became snake-like.

Looking Away

When anyone avoids eye contact, it's usually a sign of low self-esteem. The person may be uneasy with the conversation, person, or atmosphere in which they find themselves. Furthermore, anxiety in social situations can make a person fearful of locking eyes with someone they don't know. Avoiding eye contact may also be a sign of inner turmoil. Maybe they're avoiding eye contact because they're battling latent attraction impulses, or maybe they're suppressing something that makes them nervous. This does not signifies that the individual is dishonest or untrustworthy. They can be plagued by crippling self-consciousness that affects their mood.

Visual Directions

During a conversation, how we position our eyes and what we want to concentrate on can tell a lot. Glancing downward, for example, may mean embarrassment or even submission. When children are reprimanded, they often look down to demonstrate their contempt for their behavior.

Internal discomfort is also shown by sideways glances. When a coworker you hate comes into the room, for example, you might instinctively look at them sideways because they are the bane of your life. This can also happen when you communicate with people who irritate you. The implication of the sideways stare is disappointment. You may give someone the side-eye if you see anything that isn't quite right or if they are being sly. This reflects a complete dislike for their demeanor, prestige, and even their facial expressions.

Many people equate squinting with a loss of vision. Although this is real, a squint may also be used to convey disbelief or uncertainty. Someone can overhear something and want to know more. As a result, they squint their eyes while listening, almost as if to say, "I don't believe you... I need more information!"

Stress can cause rapid blinking, which can send a person into a tizzy. You might see someone blinking rapidly when rushing to complete a mission. Sweating or trembling can accompany this. Excessive blinking, on the other hand, may be a subtle indication of arrogance. When a supervisor speaks to an employee, for example, he or she can blink rapidly in an effort to dismiss the conversation. The supervisor is effectively blinded from the employee for less than a second by this quick blinking, suggesting that they would rather be doing something else.

Extreme attraction is demonstrated by a direct look coupled with a lowered lid and head. It's almost like a "come hither" invitation among friends. Sexual desire heightens this gaze, which may also cause pupil dilation.

Attention Deficiency and Failure to Concentrate

The span of time it takes the body to concentrate on one point after it has been subjected to intense movement is known as eye nystagmus. People with nystagmus that lasts longer than 14 seconds can have trouble staying concentrated. One academic facility evaluates a child's nystagmus precision by rotating them many times and making them look up at the ceiling. The eyes then shift quickly, dilating and then narrowing. The longer it takes for the child to recover, the more information is gathered. They continue to do this spinning exercise on a weekly basis in the hopes of improving their ability to stay concentrated on one task despite several distractions. Their eyes can stabilize in a shorter period of time as their tolerance grows. The aim is to improve their ability to ignore external disturbances, which will aid in the treatment of attention deficit disorder. The movement of a child's eyes informs qualified professionals how much help he or she may need and in what field. Aren't the eyes stunning?

Our eyes open the door to several self-discoveries. With only a glance, you will gain a psychological insight on how you view yourself and others! Paying close attention will show frustration, lust, attraction and even doubt. Since the eyes have a clear link to the brain, it's only logical that they're the soul's gatekeepers. You will have the grand ability to evaluate an individual in a complex manner if you integrate these fast tips into your social life. Detecting deception is, of course, a feature of the eyes. If we continue on our journey through body language, we will soon discover how an individual's eyes can show their trustworthiness.

Meaning of Body Posture

The way you sit and stand when interacting with others can communicate a great deal about you to them without you or them being conscious about it. If you somehow find that statement a bit vague, consider this: have you ever felt "suspicious" of someone who looks nice, talks nice, and smells nice? I mean despite the "nice" appearance, have you ever felt that deep inside, this actually may be a dubious character that's just trying to put one over you? If you have, then you may not have been aware of it, but you were actually able to pick up on his or her body language—particularly their body positions—on a subconscious level. Through their posture, you were also able to somehow pick up on what they're really about on a subconscious level. Eventually, you can also succeed in your relationships and in your career or business life.

Let's take a look at some of the most common positions that contribute to your body language.

Sitting Positions

A lot of people—maybe you included—aren't aware but the way we sit can tell others much about how we're feeling at the moment or even our current mood, as well as our personality. The way we sit can actually project a shy or insecure vibe or project a more confident, even aggressive one. Let's take a look at these sitting positions.

The Cross-Legged Position

For the most part, sitting with legs crossed projects a feeling of being carefree and open. Crossing the legs with knees spread to the side can actually give people the subconscious impression that physically, you're all game to take on new ideas, which can also be subconsciously perceived to mean that emotionally speaking, you're also open to some new things. Being open means you're a person that's fun and interesting to be with, which can actually make more people be drawn to you naturally.

The Erect Sitting Position

Without thinking much about it, it's also easy to see that a person who usually sits this way is a confident, reliable, and secure one. And if you sit this way most of the time, regardless of if consciously or unconsciously, people will think of you as such a person. And this's a great thing to have, especially when it comes to doing business with others. This is because if people think you're actually reliable and secure, they'll more easily trust you to do business with you. Don't even get me started on how this will help you with dating or love.

The Reclined Sitting Position

Of all the sitting positions, this one's perhaps the one that can give you a Big Bang Theory vibe, i.e., an analytical one. Leaning back is a gesture that simply shows you're able to properly think about or observe situations without necessarily or hastily acting upon them. This also means you may be more objective than most other people being able to separate yourself enough from a situation to think about it first before taking action. And from a relational perspective, this can give others the impression that you're a person who's very much aware of how others feel, which can also help you connect to people on a deeper level and easily earn their trust and loyalty.

Crossed Ankle Sitting Position

In most cases, sitting with ankles crossed simply gives others the impression that the person sitting in this position isn't only elegant and refined but is also humble and open-minded. Coupled with slightly open legs, this position conveys a feeling of being comfortable both under one's own skin and in the environment.

Clutching Armrests Sitting Position

Sitting stiffly and are practically clutching at the chair's armrests shows awareness of and sensitivity to one's surroundings. And by clutching on armrests, the seated person comes across to most other people as emotionally and physically insecure because of the need to clutch on to the chair's armrests for stability most of the time.

But merely using the armrests by resting your arms on them instead of actually clutching to them can also give a much different impression—an opposite one in fact. Doing so can communicate that you're a stable person—emotionally, physically, and mentally—so much that people are predisposed to depending on you for their own emotional and intellectual stability. You'll likely become their figurative armrests.

Crossed Arm Sitting Position

Oftentimes, crossed arms are perceived as indicators of confidence, defensiveness, and strength. But it can also be taken as an indicator of being closed to new ideas or being protective of one's self, with arms crossed in front of the body being taken to mean as protection of one's body from the rest of the world. Either way, a crossed arm sitting position is actually a body language that says a person is neither open nor weak.

Sidesaddle Sitting Position

If you're a lady, then this one's for you specifically. The amazing sidesaddle sitting position is one where you sit with your knees to the side. This type of sitting position basically communicates a naturally sweet, caring, and delicate personality. And oh...it can also communicate a personality that's a wee bit flirtatious. So, choose wisely to whom you'll show this particular body position. And when you point your knees and chest to the other person, it can be subconsciously taken as being available and open to something new, i.e., a possible relationship.

Hands on Lap Sitting Position

When your hands are on your thighs and are still, it can be construed as a sign that you're a thoughtful and shy person. Also, you can come across as a calm and collected person if you're actually able to keep your hands still while sitting down.

Dead Center Sitting Position

Sitting smack in the center of a couch, bench, or even table communicates to others that you're a totally confident person. Why? It's because people who aren't confident, i.e., insecure or even tentative, tend to worry about where to sit down—they practically fuss over where they should sit and sit in the center is very uncomfortable for most of them. So, by sitting in the middle, it essentially communicates to others that you're not afraid of being in the center of attention and that you can choose to sit anywhere you want to. And by subtly communicating to others that you're confident, you can also come across as friendly and bold, which can make it easier for you to establish rapport with others, which's a crucial skill for business.

Legs on Chair Arm Sitting Position

This is a sitting position that's mostly taken by men as it also makes use of the spread legs position. This sitting position is also one where a person stakes his ownership of the chair and communicates an aggressive and informal attitude.

While it's not unusual to see this sitting position among two friends who're whiling time away joking and laughing with each other, it's not appropriate for other, more serious situations. For example, you're a boss and your subordinate comes to you after making a big mistake at work, which's totally ok with you. Say your subordinate felt really bad about the mistake and he sits in front of your table with head held low and hands on his knees—a submissive body language. Let's say after listening for a while to what your subordinate has to say, you quickly adopt a leg-on-chair-arm position. By doing so, you've just subtly communicated to your subordinate that you don't care how he's feeling and that you're wasting your time. It's as if you're telling him you're tired of the same old story. Through this position, you're actually coming off as aggressively dismissing your subordinate's feelings.

Now maybe the reason you're dismissing your subordinate's feelings is actually a very good one: that you don't think he's done anything seriously wrong and that he shouldn't feel that bad about his mistake. Now even if you verbally communicate that, remember how powerful body language can be when it comes to communicating with others—about how it's more powerful than verbal communications. Therefore, even if you meant well and really wanted to encourage him, your body language, i.e., the legs-on-the-chair-arm position, essentially communicates a vastly different message; one that aggressively says you're not interested in how he feels and that he's just wasting your time.

On your end, you should actually avoid this body language at all costs, save for informal interactions with people with who you already have deep relationships. Now if you use this in a business setting, chances are high that you'll perhaps just piss off your counterparties and substantially lower your chances of being able to successfully discuss or negotiate with them and persuade them to side with you.

The Chair Straddling Sitting Position

Ages ago, it normally used to be that men used shields for protection against their enemies' weapons. These days, people use whatever's available to symbolize their attempts at protecting themselves against the perceived verbal and physical attacks. And these attempts may include hiding behind an object— such as doors, fences, or even gates, and straddling a chair.

By straddling a chair, a person is also able to symbolically protect him or herself using a chair's backside. Moreover, such a position can make a person look dominant and aggressive, which can help fend off "attackers." and because straddling a chair requires a spread legs posture, it also allows a person to take up more space and thus, adding extra assertion to the posture.

As with other dominating positions, change your position so that they'll also be forced to break theirs. For example, you can stand up and go behind him or her, which will force her to turn around and break the straddling position in order to continue interacting with you. The chances of this working are also high because by going behind the straddler, you put him or her in a vulnerable role that people with strong personalities hate.

Now, what if the straddler is sitting on a swivel chair that can also very easily turn around without having to break the straddling position? Breaking his or her perceived dominance will actually require you to add another action to changing your position: moving into his or her personal space. After standing up to continue conversing with a straddler, which also puts you in a position to look down on him or her, moving into his or her personal space will also make it very uncomfortable for him or her to continue straddling the chair, which will eventually force him or her to finally abandon the straddling position and change into something more comfortable.

Legs and Feet

Importance of Legs and Feet in Body Language

The signs made with the legs and feet are quite difficult to control consciously or even fake. The leg and feet can give clues to a person's moods and feelings.

What to consider when trying to decipher the body language of the leg and feet:

- Take note that men and women seat differently. This is the first consideration when you are reading leg body language. This is maybe partly because of clothing and partly because of sexual differences. Men obviously exhibit more open leg positions compared to women.

- More mature women tend to adopt more modest leg positions compared to younger women. This may be brought about by differences in upbringing, social trends, and types of clothing. When attempting to read and assess body language, keep these considerations in mind.

- You should also consider that when people have been sitting for long periods, they tend to shift leg positions. This may lead to making false assumptions in terms of the signals other people are making.

- Leg signals are often accompanied by hand and arm signals. For instance, you are likely to see someone with crossed legs and crossed arms. This may come off as having feelings of disinterest, insecurity, detachment, or rejection.

It is significant to take into memo that the terms "crossed legs" or "leg-crossing," when used alone, may refer to the legs crossed at both knees. The leg position known as "Figure-4" entails the supporting leg being crossed above the knee by the lower calf of the crossing leg. This creates a figure-4 shape, that's how it got its name. It is also known as the American leg cross since it is more popular in the United States than in the UK.

Upper Body and Torso

Our arms and hands play an important role in understanding body language:

- An open stance of the arms conveys sincerity and acceptance of the situation.

- A defensive stance with crossed arms across the chest may suggest skepticism or distrust about what the other person is saying.

- The open palms of the hands show a relaxed and comfortable state of mind.

- Putting your hands in your pockets is a typical sign of nervousness or disinterest.

- Rage or fury can be expressed by the hands on the waist.

The way someone shakes hands can convey a variety of messages:

- When shaking hands, it is traditional to stand up. This is a respectful gesture. Sincerity is shown by maintaining eye contact during the handshake.

- Sweaty palms suggest anxiousness or nervousness, while the person who initiates the handshake shows trust.

- A strong handshake with the hand pointing downward is generally recognized as a symbol of confidence. Often, the palms should make contact with one another. It's likely that they're compensating for something that's too tight. On the other side, a shaky handshake with the hand pointed upward denotes shyness or nervousness.

Back and Shoulders

It displays confidence when the shoulders are squared and pushed back without overtightening the back muscles.

Tension and nervousness are indicated by rigid and tense back muscles. Slouching of the back or shoulders is a sign of boredom or laziness.

Crossed Arms

Crossing arms can convey a variety of messages, but it typically portrays a protective individual. When you cross your arms, you're showing that you don't want to interact with other people or external influences. Many people behave as if they are crossing their arms because they are cold and want to create some energy. People would perceive such an expression in a similar way due to its shallowness. With all due respect, when it comes to coping with body language, this has a completely different sense.

It also means that you are not prepared to participate in any debates or discussions of this kind. This effectively creates a shield in front of the body to alert someone who is about to initiate a conversation. As a consequence, you should be careful when interacting with someone who has crossed his or her arms. Vulnerability or a sense of insecurity can influence a person's decision to cross their arms. If that's the case, it'll be taken as a sign that you're looking for self-comfort, which is understandable at this point.

Although crossing one's arms can indicate that one is closed to any arguments, there are other signals that accompany the gesture that you should be aware of. As soon as a person crosses his or her arms, he or she can follow up with a shake of the head to indicate "no" or even avoid making eye contact at all costs. Other signs could include the person's feet pointing away from you, crossed legs, and leaning backward. These are the symptoms of someone who is crossing their arms to keep people away.

Standing with Your Hands On Your Shoulders

Standing with your hands on your waist is the perfect way to show the world that you are in complete charge of your life. People who are skilled at reading body language can tell you exactly what you need to know without any ambiguity. It can also be interpreted as an offensive display. When flirting with women, men like this pose the most. They will lean slightly, which is interpreted to suggest that the man is interested in the woman and would like to keep her for a longer period of time.

This isn't to say that women don't strike the pose as well. They do, and the meaning is the same. The pose may be very different, but the hands on the hips are still present. Anything else might shift, but that isn't one of them. The person may decide to lean forward while swaying their head to one side. All of this is intended to demonstrate that you're paying attention to what's being said, and it can be complemented by a simple smile and direct eye contact.

This is a confident stance, and those who follow it are still able to go to lengths to achieve their goals. Simply stand up and put your hands on your hips if you are aggressive and want to demonstrate it nonverbally. You and your personality will be the focus of attention. It's more powerful than simply saying, "I'm violent." Actions still speak louder than words, and this body language is no different.

Hands Clasped Behind the Back

The key signals that clasping your hands behind your back can convey to other people are fear, frustration and rage. It gives the impression that a person is exposed and does not want to be seen by anyone. Any discomfort may occur, which is the most common symptom of someone who is experiencing anxiety. At the same time, you'll feel like sitting, standing, walking and running.

Arms Spreading Wide

Another motion that can give you the feeling of order is to spread your hands. You'll try to make as much room as possible available for your use. This is a gesture that will instill trust in you because it demarcates your territory. This is powerful nonverbal communication that does not require the use of words to communicate what you are feeling. When they have power to command, both men and women enjoy adopting this pose.

Expanded arms may also be viewed as a willingness to accept. People who are about to hug each other are more likely to note this. That's a great way to express your love for someone without really saying it. When it's not about love, people embrace each other as a greeting, but when it's about the same sex, it sends a somewhat different message. Also children hug each other when playing, which should not be interpreted as meaning that their acts are excessive. Extending one's arms broadly is a nonverbal contact that conveys a powerful message about one's emotions.

Arms Must Be Held in Close to the Body

There are many moments in life when holding your arms close to your body is advantageous. Some sports, such as golf and baseball, put a greater focus on arm positioning to protect the body from injury. That is one understanding of this pose, which is also important while driving a car. Holding your arms near to your body will send a serious message about your inner self, even if you are not engaging in sports. Many people have considered it to be a valuable nonverbal means of expressing their feelings.

This stance indicates that you are engrossed in yourself and do not want to draw attention to yourself. This stance causes people to withdraw from the public eye, although temporarily, in order to live a more private life. When you have any personal issues to deal with and don't want other people to get in the way, simply adopt this stance and the message will be delivered effectively.

Fidgeting or Rapidly Tapping Fingers

Do you have a habit of fidgeting or clicking your fingers quickly? You could have done so on many occasions without understanding what message you were sending to others. Many who are trained to read body language will quickly detect your impatience, boredom, or frustration. One of the ways people can alleviate stress in their bodies is to do so.

Non-Verbal Legs and Feet Signals

Signal	Possible Meaning/s	Details
Sitting position—leg direction (general)	Could be a sign of interest or attentiveness (depends on the direction of the leg).	Generally, when a person is seated, the knees are directed towards the point of interest. Conversely, the leg is likely to point away from someone (or something) that they deem uninteresting or which poses a threat. This rule applies to crossed legs—the upper knee would indicate interest or disinterest, depending on the direction it points to. The distinct and obvious the position, the stronger the attraction or repulsive feeling.
Sitting position—uncrossed legs (general)	It may indicate openness.	The open uncrossed leg position while seated generally means having an open attitude. The crossed legs position is indicative of the opposite, which may mean a closed attitude or a certain degree of caution.

Sitting position—legs parallel (mostly done by women)	May indicate a certain degree of openness.	This is common among women, maybe because of upbringing and style of clothing. It is a sign of being open to others.
Sitting position— crossed legs (general)	It may indicate a sense of caution or disinterest.	This position may be due to a variety of reasons. It could be a feeling of being threatened or feeling a little insecure or having little to no confidence at all, among others.
Sitting—crossing legs—a significant change in sitting position.	It can either indicate interest or disinterest in the direction of the crossed upper knee.	As a general rule, the upper crossed leg and knee point in the direction of one's interest. If the knee is pointed towards the direction of a person, it means that the attention is for that particular person. If it points away from an individual, it connotes disinterest or there is a perceived threat from that particular individual. Take note that the signs are more indicative upon sitting down and immediately assuming the initial position. The leg and feet signs would

		become unreliable if people have been sitting for more than 30 minutes. They will have the need to change positions to avoid discomfort.
The 4-leg cross or the American position	It is an indication of being independent and stubborn.	This position means the person is confident. The position exposes the genital region, and it makes the upper body lean back. The crossed-leg position is like a protective barrier, so this posture is known as the stubborner position than that of the "both knees leg cross."
The 4-leg cross (or American) with a hand clamp	It is an indication of resistance. It shows the person is being stubborn.	This position is a stubborner and protective version of the standard 4-leg cross. The opposite hand holds the ankle of the crossing leg, creating a more locked position, which can be a reflection of the person's current mood.
Sitting position—open legs	It is an indication of arrogance. It can also mean a feeling of being combative. Another interpretation could be	This sign is a confident dominant posture. Men who are in an open-crotch position are rarely done in formal

	the person is sexually posturing.	situations (like meetings) as this is mainly a sexual signal. This position is quite different because the "pointing" is being undertaken by the man's crotch, whose target could be anyone—a single individual or a whole audience. It is not a traditional position for females, particularly in formal situations, and definitely not when she is wearing a skirt. Regardless of gender, this position is known as a combative one since a bigger space is needed. It also makes the person look taller or bigger. Once the person opens up their arms, they will be exposed to an open position.
Sitting position—ankle lock	It can connote defensiveness.	In men, the knees could be apart (natural for men) or together (of course for women). It can also be an indication of suppressing negative emotions.
Standing position—	It can be a sign of aggression or the person	The splayed position is where the legs are parted

legs are "splayed"	is ready to take action.	widely. It usually creates a firm base foundation from which to attack or defend. Reportedly, this makes the body look wider. The hands on hips position support the interpretation.
Military "at attention" stance	This may mean being respectful.	This position is often a sign of respect— standing upright with legs straight, together, and parallel, shoulders are back with both arms on the sides. It's also a sign of subservience when a person is addressed by someone with authority.
Sitting position—legs intertwined (usually by a female)	It is often perceived as a sign of insecurity. It is also deemed as sexual posing.	People also refer to this position as the "leg twine"—tightly-crossed leg while wrapped around the other leg. Interpretation depends on the circumstances. It can be an indication of retreat and protection. But it can also be a sexual display of the muscle and firm tone of the crossed leg. How the other parts of the body are position should be

		considered.
Standing position— legs are crossed, mimicking a scissor	It can be interpreted as a sign of insecurity or submission.	It's a stance often observed in groups of people attending a party or other gathering. It is considered a defensive signal. You might observe this in people who lack confidence in themselves. It is further reinforced by a person's lack of physical and audible involvement and connection, often in social gatherings or group meetings. When legs are crossed but the arms are not, it can be an indication of a committed agreement to stand and engage. The stance can mean many different things depending on how the other parts of the body are positioned.
Standing position— knee buckle	It may mean one is under a lot of pressure.	A pronounced knee buckle is like a collapse or surrender because the person is experiencing severe stress. On the other hand, a subtle knee bend while in a standing position may mean the person is anxiously

		anticipating an uncomfortable responsibility.
Foot (or both feet) points in a particular direction	Generally, where the foot is pointing indicates the direction of interest.	Similar to the knees, the feet are likely to point to the focus of interest. Conversely, they will point away from something or someone they are not interested in them.
Standing position—foot forward	This signal may mean that the attention of the person is directed towards the dominant member of the group.	You'll often observe this position in groups. You will have an idea who is perceived as the leader of the group because people are inclined to put their foot forward towards the person the group unintentionally made the leader (if not yet the leader).
A little shoe-play (mostly seen in females)	It is a form of relaxation. It can also mean the female is flirting.	When you observe a woman making the pose, take note of how relaxed they might be feeling at that particular moment. Dangling a show from the foot, then slipping the foot in and out of the shoe actually has sexual overtones.

Body Language and Emotions

B ody language is tricky because most body positions, postures, and movements can mean different things or not mean anything, depending on the environment. To discern which body language signals are significant and which ones are not, you should learn how several basic emotions are generally expressed through various simultaneous movements. In other words, you should try and discern patterns of movements that typically accompany certain emotional states, rather than dragging yourself through the tedious, often unreliable, practice of committing to memory hundreds of individual physical actions and what the meaning of those actions might be.

Thoughtful or Focused

The states of either being thoughtful or focused are usually characterized by a person being noticeably devoid of movement. A person's stillness in this instance reveals concentration on either some unspoken string of thought (if thoughtful) or what the other person is trying to say (if focused). Occasionally, a focused or thoughtful person may perform minor movements repetitively, such as tapping a pencil against a tabletop or twiddling their thumbs. A thoughtful or focused person will unconsciously display this body language, and this body language will be present and consistent for extended lengths of time.

Some of the other body language that is indicative of a person being thoughtful or focused includes:

- Holding the head in the hands

- Consistently staring at something

- Consistently maintaining strong eye contact

- Furrowed brow

- Arms folded with a vacant stare.

- Looking up

- Laying the chin on the fingers or hand

- General absence of movement

- Tilting the head

- Leaning back in the chair

- Scratching the head

Bored

People generally become bored when they do not want to be wherever they are and do not want to be doing whatever it is that they are doing. When a person is bored and wants to go somewhere else, the body will show signs that it, too, wants to go somewhere else. The tension between wanting to leave and having to stay causes people discomfort. Therefore, bored people will generally engage in some physical activity to distract themselves from that discomfort.

Some of the common movements associated with boredom include:

- Eye rolls

- Leaning backward and forward in the chair

- Wandering eyes

- Furtive looks at objects such as a watch.

- Heavy sighing

- Staring into the distance

- Yawning

- Shifting their weight

- Foot-tapping

- Twiddling thumbs

- Finger-tapping

- Uncrossing and crossing arms

- Uncrossing and crossing legs

- Scribbling or doodling

- Playing with small objects such as paper clips, pens, coins, etc.

- Pointing the body away from the speaker

- Side-to-side head movement

- Preening clothes or fingernails

- Stretching

- Trying to do something else.

- Holding the chin in the hand and looking around the room

When people are bored, they engage in some kind of physical activity to stay attentive. If a bored person does not engage in these physical activities, they may fall asleep. Because of the necessary presence of physical activity, boredom is among the easiest emotional states to spot and among the most difficult to hide.

Some of the signs of boredom are the same or similar to those of someone attentive or thoughtful. The key distinction between the two is the absence or presence of movement. Remember that if a person is staring off into space and is completely still, they may be thinking something over. If that same person is staring off into space while fidgeting with something, odds are that person is bored out of their skull.

Angry

An angry person will express that anger by becoming withdrawn, aggressive, or defensive. Anger in the form of aggression is the easiest to spot, being characterized as a flushed face, puffed out chest, a set jaw, tight lips, and a loud and forceful voice. However, many people try not to express their anger so outwardly, or they at least try to control that expression, and will then tend to become withdrawn or defensive.

Some common signs of the three types of anger include:

- Flushed face

- Sarcastic or feigned laughter

- Irritated movement of the arms

- Crossed legs

- Crossed ankles

- Crossed arms

- Finger-pointing

- Firm posture

- Phrase repetition

- Lips that are closed tight

- Quick speech

- Quick body movements

- Fixed facial expression or grimace

- Shaking

- Clenched fists

- Set jaw

- General tension

- Quick, shallow, or short breaths

- Hands placed on hips

- Invasion of personal space

Frustrated

The two forms of frustration are surrender and confrontation. Confrontational frustration is characterized by the person who is under the impression that they can fix whatever is causing the frustration by directly approaching the problem. The signs of confrontational frustration can therefore mirror those that would otherwise indicate anger. The frustration of surrender happens when that irritated person realizes that they cannot fix whatever is irritating them. Surrender frustration is characterized, not by signs indicating anger, but by signs of passive irritation.

Some common signs of frustration of the confrontational variety are:

- Direct and consistent eye contact

- Repetition of certain phrases

- Invasion of personal space

- Shoulder shrugs

- Finger-pointing

- Hand-gesturing

Signs exhibiting the start of surrender frustration include:

- Over-emphasized movement

- Hands to head

- Scowling

- Sighing

- Quick exhalation

- Hands resting on hips

Signs that the surrender frustration has been reached include:

- Hands thrown in the air

- Shoulder shrugging

- Turning away

- Walking away

- Closing the eyes

- Rolling the eyes

- Head shaking

Although confrontational frustration can easily turn into anger, it is important that you don't confuse the two and thereby throw off your analysis. It is also important that you don't mistake boredom for surrender type of frustration. While several bored signals mirror those of surrendering out of frustration, bored people are not necessarily frustrated, just as those who have surrendered to a situation out of frustration are probably not going to be bored.

Depressed

Clinical depression is an animal all its own. Someone suffering from clinical depression may be entirely unable to function, suffer from eating disorders, find concentrating on anything almost impossible, and disregard hygiene. Clinical depression requires medical treatment. We will not here be describing clinical depression. What we mean here by "depression" is the average type of day-to-day depression that we all have felt at some point in our lives.

Depression affects almost every one of your body's functions, including your body language and voice. Depressed people move and speak differently. Someone who is depressed will be sluggish and glum. They will be wholly unenthusiastic and tired. Thus, in addition to analyzing someone's body language when searching for signs of depression, remember to pay attention to that person's voice. That is another avenue by which depression is sure to manifest itself.

Specific signs of day-to-day depression include:

- Lack of concentration
- Poor memory
- Intentional and slow movement
- Relaxed posture
- Increased appetite
- Decreased appetite
- Slow and quiet speech
- Lack of focus
- Eyes downcast

- Isolation

- Diminished capacity to plan in advance

- Lack of attention to personal hygiene

- Lack of attention to personal appearance

Nervous

Being nervous, just like being bored, causes discomfort. Again, like boredom, to distract themselves from that discomfort, a nervous individual will move their body. Being nervous creates a lot of energy, and a nervous person will need to find something to do with all that extra energy.

Signs that are typical of nervousness include:

- Body tension

- Eyes moving back and forth.

- Curling up of the body

- Rocking

- Side-to-side shifting of weight

- Uncrossing and crossing arms

- Uncrossing and crossing legs

- Tapping hands

- Tapping fingers

- Tapping feet

- Throat clearing

- Lip biting

- Nervous coughing

- Adjustment of, or fidgeting with, hair, jewelry, hands, pens, coins, clothing, fingernails, or any other small object

- Hand squeezing

- Nervous smiling (frequently and rapidly alternating between smiling and not smiling)

- Nervous talking

- Eyes downcast

- Shaking

- Biting fingernails

- Preening cuticles

- Sudden silence

- Upper body rotation from side to side

- Sweating

As you can see, nervousness comes with plenty of signs, many of which are shared with other emotional states. However, nervous people will generally exhibit more than just one of the signs listed above. Therefore, when analyzing whether someone is nervous or not, look for two or three signs to be sure you are not misreading the situation.

Embarrassed

People who are embarrassed typically conceal their embarrassment, making embarrassment a rather tricky feeling to track. Further, how someone acts when they are embarrassed varies from one person to the next. It is important, then, to understand and identify the behaviors that typify embarrassment so that you do not mistake one of those behaviors for nervousness, anger, fear, secretiveness, or defensiveness.

Common indications that a person is feeling embarrassed include:

- Averting their eyes

- Lack of eye contact

- Head shaking

- Laughing nervously

- Smiling nervously

- Flushed fact

- Leaving the situation

- Avoiding contact with others

Confused

Practically speaking, confusion rarely manifests itself independently of other emotions. A confused person will often also be showing signs of indecision, frustration, or fear. It will be useful to think of a confused person as someone who is lost in the woods and is searching for a reliable path.

Typical signs of confusion include:

- Indications of frustration

- Repetition of statements

- Fidgeting or shifting

- Picking something up then immediately setting it down

- Indications of being indecisive

- Behavior that conflicts with itself

- Inconsistent behavior

- Repetition of movements

Fear

One of the most basic feelings is terror. Fear generally starts as a surprise, and then quickly transforms into a nerve-wracking combination of nervousness and defensiveness. In the modern age, fear does not occur as frequently as, say, anxiety, but it is healthy to have an idea of what mannerisms characterize fear in case you ever need to identify it. Keep in mind that everyone reacts to fear differently, so attention will need to be paid to determine the emotion you are looking at accurately.

Signs of fear include:

- All signs of surprise

- Eyes opened wide

- Shaking

- Breathing heavily

- Placing hands over face

- Flushed face

- Holding on to others

- Putting the hands in front of the body

- Turning the body away

- Shallow and rapid breaths

- Screaming or yelling

- Paralysis

- Exaggerated swallowing

- Gulping

- Wringing the hands or holding on tightly to something

- Not breathing

- Glancing around (keeping the head twisting)

- Leaning backward

- Rapid walking

- Lip licking

- Rigid posture

- Taking slow, hesitant steps

Surprise

The amygdala's sudden adrenaline production characterizes surprise in response to unexpected stimuli (i.e., the "fight-or-flight" response). Given its sudden and unexpected nature, surprise can result from several different emotional states, including pleasure, pain, fear, and excitement. Regardless of the cause, the physical response follows the same basic formula. That is, there is some kind of rapid movement of the body accompanied by a transitory inability to control the smaller types of muscle. Once these reactions take place, a surprised person will usually take up their pre-surprised position rather quickly. The surprise response is generally the same regardless of whether the catalyst is a good or bad thing.

Indications include:

- Going wide-eyed
- Extension of the arms
- Jumping
- Screaming
- Yelling
- Gasping
- Mouth agape
- Taking backward steps if the person is on their feet
- Leaning back if the person is sitting down
- Extension of the legs

Signs of Negative Emotions

The silent signals you show might harm your business without you realizing it. We have over 250,000 facial signals and 700,000 body signals. Having poor body language could damage your relationships by sending other people a signal that you can't be trusted. They could alienate, turn off, or offend others.

Your body language needs to be held in check, and it takes a lot of time. You may not know you're doing it, most of the time, and you might damage yourself and your business.

In order to help you manage your signals, there is extensive body language and speech mistakes that you can learn to prevent. Here are 13 mistakes you need to try to avoid:

1. Too Strong or Weak Handshake

Handshakes are usually the first impression that somebody gets from you. If your handshake is too frail, it shows you aren't professional and might be new. If your handshake is too strong, it might warn them that you are too aggressive. Try to seek out a happy medium so that you can make a good impression.

2. Looking Around

Everyone has encountered somebody who constantly looked around the room while talking with you. It probably made you think they were trying to find another person to talk to. Don't be this type of person. Everybody you talk to needs to be treated with respect.

3. Not Smiling

Do you realize that smiling can actually make you feel happy? People like to believe the opposite. If you can keep a nice smile plastered on your face, you will feel confident and people will be glad to work with you. If you catch yourself wanting to make a face, turn that into a smile.

4. No Eye Contact

I used to work with a person who would immediately stare into space anytime somebody talked to them. They said it was easier for them to focus on what others were saying if they didn't look at the talker. People use many diverse communication types, but always try to smile and make eye contact. Even keeping moderate eye contact communicates interest, confidence, and will put everyone at ease.

5. Scrunched-Up Face

You might not know that having a scrunched-up face and furrowed brow might make others think you are hostile or intimidating. This can discourage a person from being open, or it can cause them to become defensive. You can verbally assure them that you support and understand what they are saying.

6. Looking at Your Phone

If you are at a public gathering, put your phone away. Everyone is addicted to their phones now, but it is very rude. Try to engage with others and stop checking your phone every five minutes. If you have an emergency, that is fine. It is a lot easier to make a connection if something isn't distracting you.

7. Slumping

A person that slumps in their seat shows that they lack confidence or energy. It is important to show some passion and allow others to know that you believe in yourself. If you are slumping or hunched over, it is sending the wrong message. If you have a strong posture, you will feel energetic and it will be a win for everyone involved.

8. Not Listening

It doesn't matter what line of work you are in. You are going to have to talk with people some time or other. The main thing that will break or make a relationship is not listening. Listening can impact your relationship with suppliers, employee performance, and sales better than other forms of communication.

9. Speaking too Fast

Blinking quickly or speaking too fast shows distrust and nervousness. Try to pause between each sentence and allow others to finish their sentences before interrupting. Eye contact is extremely important. If you have a hard time looking people in the eye, look at the middle of their forehead. It resembles eye contact without uncomfortable feelings.

10. Getting in Their Personal Space

Invading another person's personal space has detrimental effects. A good example is men seem always to invade a woman's personal space whether they know it or not. This can cause harassment lawsuits. The best space to keep between you and another person is about half a foot. Don't treat another person's space as your own.

11. Using "But"

Repeatedly using the word "but" while talking can cause problems. Most of the time, this is going to make it seem like you are trying to make up excuses or like you don't care about what another person is saying. You might say: "I am sorry that your product didn't get to you one time, but you know how the weather is." This statement doesn't show you are truly sorry. You are putting the blame on the weather rather than addressing the person's problem.

12. Not Enough Response

If you are talking with a person, be sure to listen. This means you need to smile, nod, and make eye contact. Even if you don't agree with what the other person is saying, you can always accept that you understood what they said. This is simply showing them respect. If you don't do this, you are leaving a bad impression.

Signs of Positive Emotions

Positive body language means you are approachable, interested, and open. This doesn't mean that people should use this type of body language at all times or that it is even the best group of signs that show a person is friendly, it is just a good starting point for reading positivity in yourself and others.

Becoming Too Positive

Just because you have positive body language does not mean it is good or the best way to communicate. Because we are social animals, we have many attitudes and emotions. If you try just to use one at a time, you will seem one-dimensional or fake.

Expressing attentive and positive attitudes at all times could hurt your status and reputation. People will often start to take this for granted and will dismiss this. You should give attention and care to others, but just to the people who deserve it.

This is particularly true if you want to be extra sweet to the person you're dating. How can others take care of you, if you only try to help others and dismiss yourself, you will appear shallow and boring. There won't be any excitement or tension.

Leaning Forward

When a person likes somebody, they want to get close to them. You will appear more exciting if you get closer to them. When a person leans, and especially if they are smiling and nodding, it shows that they are interested in the things that you are saying and would like you to continue.

Does this mean you always need to nod and lean forward?

No, overdoing this might cause two problems:

1. If you lean too far, you could invade their personal space and cause them to feel uncomfortable. This is another reason we lean forward when we want to intimidate an opponent. This type of lean will be more aggressive and tenser.

2. If you constantly lean and smile with everyone, you will appear like you are very eager to please. You will lower your status with others.

Compare leaning to driving. Once you press on the gas pedal, the more eager and engaged you are. If you don't press on the pedal, you will appear more distant and relaxed. Don't go toward the extreme because you will need to change your speed for each situation.

Much like with driving, the direction in which a person leans has a big impact. We will gesture and lean toward things or places we want.

Nothing to Hide

Think about a time when you were away from your friends or family for an extended period of time. How did they greet you when they saw you again? Did they spread the arms and expose their palms like they were hugging you from a distance? This positive and open gesture can warm your heart.

Even though you can't use it daily with everybody, your boss may think your mind has left you, or you have won the lottery. You can use gestures that are similar to show positive, honest, and open body language.

When the palms are faced outward, this shows a sign of honesty and willingness and is not threatening in any way. You are letting the other person know that you aren't hiding anything and that they can trust you. Here are some other signals that might help show cooperation and sincerity:

1. Smile

2. Keep your body straight to show energy and confidence

3. Keep your clothes and body open. Don't hold anything in front of you.

4. Have good eye contact. This shows you aren't afraid but are being attentive.

5. Put your hands in a position that is neutral. Never look down on them or bow to their wishes.

Stay Away from Barriers

In order to gain a person's trust, you have to make sure that you don't come off as a threat and that you don't see them as a threat. Having defensive body language can affect your attitude. If you are defensive, it is going to make it hard for other people to accept and approach you.

For this main reason, you have to keep open body language and stay away from barriers.

Your goal needs to be getting rid of your defenses and to make a confident, warm, and welcoming atmosphere. Show others that you aren't scared of them and they don't need to be afraid of you either.

This is a process, and total strangers aren't going to be your biggest fan. If you understand what steps to take, you can know their attitude toward you and speed things up.

The steps are as follows:

1. Total strangers will probably have their legs or arms crossed or possibly both. They will stay away from you. They might also hold something in front of them or button their coat.

2. As they warm up to you, you might notice their legs uncross, and other barriers disappear. They might move a bit closer to you.

3. They might begin to gesture more and show you their palms.

4. They uncross their arms.

5. They might point or lean their body toward you.

Taking the initiative could help others open up to you. We all unconsciously start to copy the body language of other people. You can reverse this process by getting into a defensive posture.

The speed of the process all depends on the culture, character, whether or not they are extrovert or introvert, and context like meeting a stranger on the street versus meeting them at a party.

How to Spot Insecurity

Many people consider enthusiastic instability as a character quality—something you're brought into the world with that fates you to a life of persistent nervousness and low confidence. Keep in mind that it can indeed feel that way to people who have been uncertain a large portion of their lives, and the genuine explanation for why we constantly feel shaky is unobtrusive: whatever caused your uncertainty, it's your propensities that keep you feeling unreliable.

In my work as an analyst, I've discovered that the ideal way to release yourself from the pattern of insecurity is to identify the propensities that are maintaining your frailty now. We as a whole have confounded lives and chronicles, yet if you need to feel not so much unreliable but more certain, taking a shot at even a couple of these propensities will have a major effect.

Shaky people have a different way of dealing with life than others. This frequently upsets their development and makes their everyday lives more difficult to manage. Here are ten things unreliable people do that crush their lives—ensure you don't have any of these characteristics!

They Live in Dread of Judgment

Shaky people always stress over what others are thinking. What's more, they don't believe they're proving to be the best. Uncertain people feel like they are always being judged, and not for who they genuinely are. This is regularly because they consider themselves the second rate and can't see how others consider them to be whatever else.

They Abstain from Meeting New People

Shaky individuals don't care about meeting new people for an assortment of reasons. They probably won't have confidence in themselves to be optimistic about social circumstances or probably won't believe they're sufficiently intriguing to hold a discussion.

They Don't Accept They're Sufficient

Uncertain people never believe they're sufficient for anything. For meeting new people, for meriting companions, for the next advancement at work. They could be the most pleasant, most entertaining, most determined individuals, but they'll never observe themselves that way. They don't think anybody can consider them to be decent, because they don't feel like they are.

They're Not Consistent with Themselves

Shaky people are the ones who frequently become everyone around them. They're similar to chameleons in social circumstances, adjusting to their environmental factors in an attempt to fit in better. They don't feel good acting naturally, so they attempt to become any other person.

They Live in a World with Disavowal

Shaky people can deny everything without exception. They don't accept realities as realities; they're ready to discount them as nothing. Even if all the signs point to a positive sign, circumstance, a shaky individual will deny everything just to remain on their bound track.

They're Destined to Fizzle

Because shaky people have no confidence in themselves, they're bound to come up short. They never siphon themselves for advancement at work, and they can't develop enough certainty to hit on that adorable outsider at the bar. Rather than merely gulping their nerves and going for any fantasy, they think about the most noticeably terrible things and demand that they're bound to fizzle. They're so certain about this result that they won't even attempt.

They Don't Trust in Others

Uncertain people don't trust in themselves; however, they don't trust in others, either. They are frequently suspicious, feeling that every other person is making a decision about them or out to get them. They don't believe they can have companions because they don't believe they're significant people. They can't have a relationship because they feel their partner is an accomplice in undermining them and deceiving them.

They Search for the Most Exceedingly Awful

Uncertain people can't locate the positive side of any circumstance because they're always searching for the most exceedingly awful. Even at best, they're not able to relinquish negative feelings. This frequently implies they'll destroy a circumstance to substantiate themselves right and demonstrate that the world is truly giving them the most exceedingly awful of each circumstance.

They're Not Established in Reality

Shaky people aren't established. They regularly live in their minds, which is the reason they're distrustful and don't trust in others. They come up short on the rationale that demonstrates they are respectable people, rather deciding to face a daily reality such that they are frequently the people in question, never trusted, not worth love or companionship, never going to climb the professional bureaucracy. As a general rule, this individual is gifted and mindful, but since they can't remove themselves from their instabilities, they're not ready to work in reality.

They Pass Up the Best of Life

Shaky people invest an excess of energy in their own heads. They put themselves down, thinking the most exceedingly awful of themselves as well as other people. By living in this antagonism, they're passing up the best of life. They're not ready to see the positive qualities in the people around them or the excellence in their day-by-day lives.

How to Spot a Liar

Everybody can tell a lie. Most people do. Most Americans will tell a couple of lies per day. There are ways that you can spot these lies.

The best way for a lie to be spotted is by knowing how a person will likely act when they speak the truth. Ask a person a simple question like: "Where are you from?" Now, you have to watch what their eyes do and how their voice sounds.

These signs aren't foolproof. If a person is uncomfortable, they might fidget in their seat. If they are nervous, their voice might crack.

There has been a lot of discussion in the medical community, especially in the mental health community, about which body language cues may reveal when someone is lying. Our perceptions can keep up from correctly interpret signs that we see. It is tough to be able to figure out people by watching their body language because a person might look uneasy or tense for various reasons. It's easy to think that someone who won't make eye contact is automatically lying. They might not be lying, but might be feeling ashamed, bored, or anxious. We aren't as great at reading others as we think we are.

Even though it might be clear that everybody lies, it is clear that there are certain people who can tell a lie easier and more than others. During this study, the "champ" had told 46 lies in just one week which equaled to about seven per day. You may be thinking who these people are who are capable of lying even more than the rest of society. These are people who are used to lying every day. Do these people have specific personality traits? What were their genders? What age were they? Does telling a lie have a connection to their relationships?

Personality of Liars

During the diary studies, every person filled out some personality measures.

That information was then used to see if specific personality types were prone to tell more lies.

When we went through the questions "who lies?" did a specific type come to mind? Was your guess that people who lie more were more scheming and manipulative? If so, you need to keep your intuition handy. People who are manipulative are more apt to lie than those who aren't manipulative.

Manipulative people usually only care about one thing, and that is themselves, so you may think that liars don't care about anyone else. This isn't entirely true. People who lie frequently could also care too much about others. The thing they care about most is what others care about them. These people worry about what impression they make on others: "If I do this, will they think I'm a loser?" or "If I say this, what will she think?" These people have the personality type of impression-management. This person will tell many, many lies. What is interesting is these people actually know they are lying, and they know they do it more than others. This is worth noting because the diary study participants thought that they were more honest than others.

Extroverts also lie more. This is why we needed to keep track of their social interactions and not just the lies. If just the lies were counted, extroverts would be able to lie more than introverts since they spend a lot of time around people. This looks at lying rates or how many lies people told according to their opportunities. Extroverts did tell lies more than introverts, even though the difference wasn't substantial.

So, why do extroverts lie more than introverts? It is the little lies that make social interactions go a lot smoother. Extroverts know about being nice, and they practice this as often as they can, so they don't realize just how much they actually lie. Evidence has been found that most college students don't realize they are lying. When the extroverts were asked to take a look at how many lies they told during the last week, it was surprising to find out how much they had actually lied. The reason behind why extroverts lie more isn't really clear.

Frequent Liars and Relationships

For those who had participated in the study mentioned above, they had to rate the quality of their relationship with those of the opposite sex and with those of the same sex. They show how enduring, satisfying, and warm their relationships were, how well their friends and they understood each other, and how fast they could make friends.

Their quality of relationships with those of the opposite sex didn't correspond with the rate at which they lied. It was the opposite for relationships of the same sex. Those who had good relationships with those of the same sex didn't lie as much, especially those self-serving lies, as those who were in bad relationships with people of the same sex.

Women and Men: How They Compare

On average, with every type of lie, women and men are equal in their tendency to lie. Once they looked closer at the various types of targets and lies, this is when the differences showed up.

Think about two types of lies: kind-hearted and self-serving.

Kind-hearted lies are told solely to make someone else feel or seem better, or to protect them from being hurt, humiliated, blamed, or disciplined. Consider the following statements:

- "I know how you feel!"

- "What a wonderful meal!"

- "You look wonderful!"

How to look at these four combinations of targets and liars:

- Women telling lies to women.

- Women telling lies to men.

- Men telling lies to women.

- Men telling lies to men.

In three of the above, people will tell more self-serving lies than kind-hearted ones. In the other one, people tell the same amount of self-serving and kind-hearted. Which one, you ask?

Kind-hearted lies are exchanged between women more. If men were involved, either as targets or liars, the self-serving lies always prevailed. There were always two to eight times more self-serving than kind-hearted lies.

Age and Lying

The community people didn't lie as much as college students. So, this means that older adults don't tell as many lies, right? Not really, the people in the community were different in other ways, too. There was 81% that was employed, and 34 percent only had a high school education.

In a different study, adults were asked how much they had lied in the past 24 hours. They saw that as their age got higher, the number of lies they told was a lot lower. But they didn't include how many opportunities they had to lie.

This isn't for certain, but it could be that as we get older, we lie a lot less.

Types of Lying

If you begin researching how to know if somebody is lying, you are going to find many articles that are going to give you lists that include averting eye contact, fidgeting, changes in voice, and nervousness. If you've ever been on a job interview, you've probably experienced this. These are typical reactions to stressful circumstances.

Spotting lies is hard to do. Everybody exhibits various idiosyncrasies when lying instead of a set pattern that is consistent for everyone. If somebody lies during an interview, it could be likely that most of what they said is true. It is hard to go through all the information and find out which parts are deceitful while conducting an interview.

Lying is hard to do, too. A person who is knowledgeable and skilled knows how to see and expose lies by using detailed inquiries. You could ask the exact same question in different ways to get information that is more accurate. You can constantly rephrase that question until you get all the clarification you want. If someone is lying, constantly pushing the conversation might lead to a new choice; they will have to either escalate the lie or say they don't understand and that they don't tell you the truth. If they decide to escalate the lie, indicators of lying will be more obvious.

Understanding the various kinds of lies could be helpful when recognizing the problems that a liar might go through whether friend or foe. Knowing the kinds of lies to watch out for could be helpful when trying to detect lies:

Compulsive Lying

This is caused by a person having the need for attention and low self-esteem. A compulsive liar will find it hard to stop lying. They will tell their lies even if telling the truth would have been better and easier. Most people believe that every word of what they say is the truth. They live in a world that is different from reality. It isn't ridiculous; it is tragic.

White Lies

This type of lie is considered the less serious of all. People claim they tell white lies just to be polite or tactful. It might be just making up excuses for not attending a party or not showing appreciation for a gift you don't want. Constantly telling white lies could cause some conflict because, after some time, they can cause problems with others because they will start to realize the insincerity. This is what causes people who tell white lies to lose their credibility.

Saying that you have something to do when you don't just so that you don't have to let them know that you don't want to go out with them can hurt as much as a straight lie and saying that you are fine even when you feel down or sad can hurt you more than the other person. When you tell this little white lie, you are disrespecting the person who asked a simple question to help build the relationship. It puts up roadblocks when building a deep relationship.

Broken Promises

This is failing to keep a promise or commitment. It creates a lot of damage when a person makes promises that they never had any intention of keeping. Saying that you will do something that you know you aren't going to be able to do can cause a lot of problems.

What many people don't realize is that lying and breaking a promise creates double damage. It causes hurt feelings that didn't have to happen. Breaking promises hurts the hope of others. They get excited because you said you could do it just to have their hopes destroyed when you don't. These broken promises could easily lead to lives getting broken.

Deception

People who deceive create impressions that cause other people to get misled by creating false impressions or not telling all the facts. You might not like for others to think you are smart. You joke about being smart to try to make people think that you aren't smart. It might work sometimes. It might not feel like you are lying. You think you are pretending to be something you aren't. Being deceptive is hurtful. It is very subtle but deadly at the same time. It's like when you are a child, and you exaggerate about everything you can do even when knowing you can't. You make yourself look more successful, experienced, better, and greater.

Fabrication

This is telling other things that you aren't sure are true. These are very hurtful because they can lead to rumors that could damage other's reputation. When you decide to start a rumor about someone, it isn't just a lie, but you are stealing other people's reputations. Some people love to spread rumors. They like to tell lies about a person you don't like. It works most of the time. You are deliberately making false stories up.

Body Language of a Child

First, we are required to talk about why it is different to read a child's body language. The first explanation is that they are still young and have not yet mastered emotional self-control. Children cry when they are sad. They will smile if they are happy. They yell and make furious expressions when they are angry, and they cover their faces when they are embarrassed as their cheeks get red. Some kids may even choose to express the emotions they are experiencing to you. Children have no reason to hide their struggles because they are still learning about the world.

Children's body language is particularly simple to read as a result. They are unable to understand how to control their emotions, therefore they consistently express their feelings. When you read a child's emotions, you are reading what they actually feel.

Children's inability to conceal their emotions as well as their ignorance of the body language cues they exhibit make it vital to keep this in mind while interpreting their body language. They lack the ability of adults to communicate the opposite of how they feel. Their lack of awareness of their own body language can also make it easy to spot when a child is lying. A youngster may attempt to conceal the truth through their words, but because they lack the mental capacity to do so in their body language as well, they frequently enable signals that they are not telling the truth or are omitting some of the truth to get through.

For instance, my sister's five-year-old daughter likes to smuggle cookies with chocolate chips before supper. Before starting to prepare dinner, my sister usually makes sure to check the Chips Ahoy packaging so she can detect any missing cookies. She will continue to question her daughter in the hopes that she will come clean on her own. Most of the time, my niece will attempt to lie about it (my personal favorite being when she claimed her father ate the cookie). She may think she sounds convincing, but there is one obvious sign that she is lying: a broad smile on her face. She smiles as she is so proud of her deceit since she believes she is getting away with something so naughty. This smile is typically followed by another sign, such as her lowering her head and gazing at the floor out of humiliation at being discovered, when it is obvious that she will not get away with it.

Everyone has a physical tell that gives them away when they are lying. Fortunately for parents, guardians and teachers, children are unable to hide their talking until they are older and have more experience both with lying and reading their own body language.

Today we know how simple it is to read the body language of a child, let's look into how important it is to pay attention to the signals a child is conveying. Whether you are around children a lot or not, you need to be able to read a child's body language so that you can do your part in ensuring that our children are healthy and safe. We can also use the body language of a child to decide whether they are in any danger, just like reading an adult's body language can help us determine whether they are in a dangerous situation. The unlucky truth is that we live in a world in which people will abuse, kidnap, and otherwise harm children. We want to help children out of such situations, but it can often be hard to tell when something suspicious is going on.

Reading a child's body language can help us determine if there is more to the statement than meets the eye. Since young children lack the ability to regulate their body language, any discomfort they feel around a particular adult will manifest itself in the way they carry themselves around that person. For instance, if a child exhibits such body language as standing stiffly, hunching their shoulders forward to make themselves smaller, or avoiding eye contact with everyone, including the adult they are with, it could mean that they are afraid of something. If they flinch whenever the adult that they are with reaches over to touch them, it could very well mean that this fear stems from someone hurting them on a regular basis, most likely this adult. Also, suppose they refuse to initiate physical contact with this adult while still never wandering any significant distance from them. In that case, it could mean that they are afraid to have any intimacy with this adult and of doing anything to anger them.

Mind you, none of this is a reason to call the police or Child Protective Services on someone. After all, there are multiple interpretations of any given body language. Standing stiffly, hunching their shoulders forward, or avoiding eye contact, for example, could just mean that the child is not comfortable in that particular environment or with strangers. Flinching and avoiding initiating physical contact with the adult could indicate, rather than fear, that the child has a problem with physical touch overall or that they are mad with that adult for some reason. Not wandering far from the adult, even though it is natural for a child to want to explore, could simply show that the child is well behaved or not particularly comfortable with checking out their surroundings on their own.

Like with all body language reading, what a child's body language means often depends on the context. If you know the child and adult personally, it can be easier to determine what the child's body language means. If they are complete strangers, it will be trickier. Nevertheless, spotting such body language in a child will help you to be on alert so that if suspicion arises that the child is being abused or has been kidnapped, you will be ready to take action.

Reading a child's body language will also help you to be there for them emotionally. If you have a child or take care of a child for large amounts of time, they will consider you their support system. They need you to help them learn about their lives and the world around them. It includes learning how to handle their emotions.

Sometimes, a child might have an emotion that they do not yet know how to explain. They may express this feeling through body language but still feel frustrated when they are unable to put their experience into words.

As an adult who distinguishes how to read body language, you can help in this situation. You can read the non-verbal cues that the child is portraying and use them to help the child express his or her feelings verbally. It will help the child learn about their feelings and more about who they are. It will also help the child grow up knowing that feelings are healthy and that it is okay to share your struggles with those close to you. If you can help your child in this way and teach these things to your child at a young age, they will have significantly fewer emotional struggles over the course of their life. This understanding is important to any adult who deals with children, such as doctors, teachers, and parents dealing with other kids, such as their children's friends.

Parents and caregivers must teach their children how to express their own body language. Still, they need to teach the kids about simple body language reading techniques. You might not want to call it body language reading to them because they either will not understand or will think the topic is boring, but this skill must be taught to children in whatever creative way necessary.

You might wonder why I believe it is important for children to be able to read body language since it is a science-based topic that can be complicated at times. We will explain why this is important now.

First, if your children understand that non-verbal communication has just as much meaning as the words they speak, they will understand the people around them at a new level. Take their time on the playground, for example. If they ask a friend to play with them and the friend says no, but is looking at the ground and has another child staring at them as if to tell them not to play with the child, they will know that there is more meaning behind this situation. They will either be able to speak up for their friend and encourage them to do what they want, or they will be deprived of worrying about what other people think or be able to walk away without feeling offended because they know that there was more to the conversation than a simple denied request to play. It might even be a mark that the friend was bullied away from playing, and your child will be able to express to a trusted adult what they saw.

Also, think about if your child sees a classmate that is not saying much when they usually talk all day, every day. If your child is aware of the body language of the people around them, they might notice this difference in behavior and ask the child what is wrong. It could make a profound change in the said child's day.

You might even consider the friendships that the child already has. As an adult, you know that being able to read simple body language allows you to have better friendships. It makes sense, then, that the same is true with friendships among children.

Your child will also be able to avoid being a bully better if they are aware of their own body language. They will understand that actions like rolling the eyes or walking away from someone when they are talking to them hurt just as much as mean words. They will understand these actions and avoid them to be nice to the people around them when other children might accidentally hurt their friends with actions like these without knowing the consequences.

When a child knows body language, they are able to make sure that their friends are comfortable with them. If the child is sitting near a friend, they will be able to say whether or not the friend is comfortable with close contact. The child would realize that the best thing is to walk away if the friend is not tolerable and shows signs of being uncomfortable.

A lot of these types of body language are things that children learn through real-life experience. The only problem with this is that real feelings are getting hurt if they are learning in real life, and real friends are feeling uncomfortable. The sooner a child acquires these skills, the sooner they can use body language to their advantage.

PART II.

How to Exploit Body Language?

Decoding Hidden Messages of Dating

There are many non verbal signals that show the different levels of intimacy between two individuals. Having a solid understanding of these signals is key in making the relationship work.

First, we'll take a look at what we've learned from your non verbal cues before and why it might not be very intentional. Then you'll see how you can break down the barriers that might exist between two people in personal conversation or in social interactions with more than one person.

Non verbal communication is the part of communication that does not require words. Some of the most important information that we convey by bouncing non-verbal messages off of other people are our body language and our tone.

We communicate so much by mimicking, bending, gesturing, and emulating to make sure that we are understood. It's a means for us to get data about a person by putting ourselves in their shoes. A person sees you walking toward him or her so they have to know what you want them to do; you must communicate with them through your movement, gestures, and pace.

Understanding the non verbal cues that each person is giving is important to a healthy relationship between two people. Non verbal signals are important because they are a more obvious, simple way for people to communicate with one another. However, they can be misconstrued and misinterpreted.

In dating, a person communicates with many different people from all walks of life, not just the person that they are interested in. This is why it's important to know how to interpret non verbal communication so that you can interact with these different types of people.

The body language that a person sends out shows their true feelings toward others and helps them pick up on the feelings of others as well. Some non verbal cues are intentional and some happen by accident. For example, being in a conversation that is stressful or annoying can cause a person to act out physically; he or she might begin tapping their fingers on the table or crossing their arms tightly across their chest when they aren't talking or making eye contact with the other party. Other people might look away when a person appears to be upset.

When two people are in love they are able to read each other's non verbal cues and pick up on body language. This is why it is vital in any relationship for two people to be able to have a conversation with one another without the need of words. This is because words can send things across that aren't truly meant, or mean things that are not true and can lead to misunderstandings.

When two people haven't spent much time together, there can be some confusion as to what non verbal signals mean in regards to dating. Here are common non verbal signs in dating:

Head Tilted Exposing Neck

This non verbal signal can be given by men or women to show a little bit of submission to someone they are interested in. The person that is doing the tilting shows that they are open minded and comfortable with the person they are with. There is a high chance that this person is looking for something more than just friendship in their relationship with you..

Eyes Closed or Half Closed

This is often mistaken for boredom, but it can also be a sign of attraction depending on other non verbal cues that are being shown by the person. If you find yourself in a conversation that seems otherwise casual where the other party is looking off into space this could be a sign of attraction in addition to any other signals shown.

Tilting The Head Up Or Down

This non verbal sign can mean that the person wants to be seen by you. If a person is making slight movements like this, it can be a way for them to look at you and show their interest in you. This is also when they are opening up more about what they are feeling toward you.

Blink Rate Slows

This is a common signal that is shown by people when they are interested in someone. When a person blinks once or twice slowly it is possible that the other person's attention makes them very comfortable and gives off signals of wanting to be around you. This is also an indication of interest in the relationship so if you see this go for it!.

Rapid Eye Movement

This can mean that the person does not have control over their emotions, which can be a good thing as a sign for pursuing social engagement. You should take this non verbal cue as you mean it and follow up to see if there might be more to what they are saying in terms of feelings toward another person.

Sleepy Eyes

If a person is showing sleepy eyes it can mean that they are tired of the situation or have a lack of interest in the conversation. This gives off signs that a person is bored with the topic or conversation, or may be bored by your general presence.

Smiling Too Much

When someone smiles a lot they want to appear happy, but it can be a sign of deception. When someone smiles too much and seems to be faking their emotions they do not feel comfortable around you. If you want to know what the other person really thinks about you, look at their eyes when they interact with you. This way you can see if they are really interested in what you are saying and where the conversation is going.

4. Blushing Cheeks

Cartoonists and visual artists are among the world's greatest readers of nonverbal cues and body language. Why do they have such a knack for depicting human action in drawings? And when they're not painting, they're paying attention to how people act in any situation imaginable. They are actually analyzing ordinary people's body language. They know what they're doing.

For example, if you're watching a cartoon and the girl mouse meets the boy mouse for the first time, you can tell some things that are about to happen right now. The first thing she'll do is begin to flutter her eyes. Then what? She'll clench her fingers and gently drive her wrists and palms outward and down.

Blushing cheeks suggest embarrassment and, on rare occasions, frustration. Sexual arousal and desire may also be shown by them. Things are going really well when you see this on your date's face and cheeks.

Steady Eye Gazing

If a person is looking you in the eye and they are not blinking this can mean that they are interested in you. Sometimes this non verbal cue can also mean that the person is being truthful about what they are saying. If the person looks away from you, it could mean their words are not true. .

Leaning Forward

This can mean that the person is interested in what you have to say and is looking forward to the topic or conversation. Leaning forward also shows that a person might want to hear more information about the topic or get closer to your face. This can be a good non verbal cue that the person is interested in you.

Eyebrow Raising

Raised eyebrows show that a person might be surprised by what you are saying. This signal shows some kind of surprise or shock towards something they are hearing. It could also mean that they are not sure if what you are saying makes sense, so they raise their eyebrows to try and figure it out better.

Space Between Fingers

Fingers placed close together are a sign of an open person, while fingers spaced out show that the person is feeling comfortable and has a sense of security in what they are saying or telling someone.

Shoulder Down and Forward

If a person's shoulders are slumped forward it is possible that they are not comfortable with what you are saying or the conversation you are having. This can also be a sign of defensiveness or hiding something in regards to your conversation.

Hand Smash or Pinching Nails

This sign can be used to show that someone is nervous about what they are saying or doing. Hiding one's hands is common but it could be a sign of lying through your teeth and trying to get away with whatever it is they have done wrong.

High-Status or Successful Body Language

Now I will show you different high-status body language positions and principles.

First of all, understand that as a high-status man, you will always make yourself comfortable first, wherever you go. That's not selfish behavior, since it will give everyone else around you the permission to relax, feel good and be comfortable too.

1. Take Up More Space

In an awkward way, low-status individuals appear to make themselves small, invisible, sitting, or standing. They don't put their energies out into the world because they don't see themselves as people of high status: they're not worth it in their minds.

They're closed on themselves; they're hiding from the outside world.

On the other hand, you're going to think that your energy is so important that, of course, you're going to be willing to share it with the world, so that you free up and take up more space.

Spread your legs and be relaxed with your weapons!

You may ask, why is that so? It's because shy and unconfident people are more concerned about what people will say. They're too afraid of "offending" people or getting really bad comments about them like they're insensitive, arrogant, or being chutzpah-tic.

If you've been paying attention, you'll remember that these are the three most common misunderstandings about trust that discourage most men from even considering being confident. This is a condition known as "people pleasing."

A great power pose is to stand over a table with your hands flat on the table and arms spread, leaning a little forward. Sitting back and spreading your arms is another one, folding your hands behind your head. Sitting with long legs and open arms is yet another one. The "superman" power pose involves standing with your legs slightly wider than your shoulders and your hands on your hips and your arms out at your sides.

In fact, these large, open and confident poses have been shown to stimulate testosterone production in both males and females. Testosterone helps decrease cortisol and increase the development of serotonin—the "happy hormone." It also contributes to an increase in confidence.

Before taking mock work interviews that they were unaware of being staged, tests were performed by making people perform these power poses for two minutes. For 2 minutes prior to such an interview, another group was asked to keep a closed-off, insecure pose.

It was found from the results of the interviews that the individuals who kept insecure poses were not less eligible candidates for the job, but because of their quiet or withdrawn manner, they were noted as being fewer desirable candidates.

Two minutes before the interview, the individuals who had kept power poses were noted as being engaging, optimistic, a pleasure to speak to, as well as interesting and desirable enough to be asked for a second interview or offered a job.

2. Do Not Hide Your Crotch

Dominant men who attract a lot of ladies have no trouble showing the world their sexuality.

So, when you are sitting, do not be afraid to draw attention to the crotch region of your body. Open your legs, maybe place a hand in that region to attract attention there subconsciously; showing a nice belt can also support you.

You are proud of who you are, aren't you?

Are you not proud of your body and your extremely energetic, sexy desire to have sex?

It's George Clooney here. He simply knows, as you can see, how to expose his crotch!

3. Slow Down Your Movements

Move slower!

Low-status people move quickly and fidgety, they're not comfortable, they don't believe in themselves.

From now on, you'll cut your movements in half.

Running, turning your back, and shifting your body around can all be done at a slower pace than you are now.

Why do you feel the need to move slowly? Knowing that you're doing it on your own terms: your time, your way and your call, is a big part of being positive.

So, when you don't have any deadlines and have all the time in the world, how do you usually go about your business? That's right—you're not in a hurry! You take your sweet time. You're relaxed.

When you're not in control, guess what—someone or something else is!

When that happens, you don't call the shots, and oftentimes, you're hurrying things up because you're dancing to other people's music. You almost always don't have as much time as you'd like to finish your assignment or responsibility. And when you don't have much control over your life, your confidence plummets. And moving very quickly all the time sends the vibe that you're not in control. And that's not confident or sexy.

The first reason for moving slowly is all about showing authority over one's self and the other is about authority over others, be it people or circumstances, as manifested by results.

Moving and speaking slower also lets you get to the root of what your true interests are so that you can put them into the world and share them with others.

"Think fast and speak slowly," as the saying goes.

4. Be Non-Reactive

Don't react to something outside of your reality. Do not turn your head while you are talking to a girl and you hear a siren or a crash. Keep centered on her and your masculine, dominant influence will be felt by her. She's not going to look at the source of the noise, and she's going to sit right here, following your high-status actions.

Being reactive in a situation may also lead to additional problems or complications. On the other hand, responsiveness ensures you remain grounded in your core sense of self-conviction and trust. Because of some situation, you may feel emotions activated inside you, but you allow them to move through you or channel them in some other way rather than get carried away in thought, verbal or physical reaction by them. When you're receptive, you take your time to thoughtfully and properly react to a circumstance or stimulus. You gain the opportunity to deal with difficult circumstances with ease, command and a sense of humour.

Also, be aware of your fidgety gestures and correct them: either you're also touching your hands when you're talking to her, or you're shifting your feet as a sign of anxiety. Stop doing that. Be still and relaxed.

With all due respect to women, being a very reactive person is so girly. Nothing else screams "girly man" than being reactive. So why does being reactive scream to a hot woman that you're more feminine than her?

I'd like you to think of a time when most things, if not everything in your life, was going as planned. How'd you feel? You probably felt great, steady, calm, or at peace. In short, you feel really confident. When one or two curve balls come your way, you're too peaceful to react inappropriately. You react in a calm and collected manner because you know that in the grander scheme of things, you're in control of your life and one or two mishaps won't change that fact.

Now think of a time when most things, if not everything in your life, wasn't going your way. How did you feel? Among many other things, I bet you felt you have no control over your life and your situation, which made you high-strung too.

Try not to be reactive. If you're not yet that confident, don't worry. You can control your impulses and if you do that long and often enough, you'll be able to reprogram your subconscious mind that you really are confident and non-reactive, which will enable you to unconsciously and naturally act that way all the time.

5. Lean Back!

For the most part, learn to lean back.

Note that leaning in is an act of very low status. Learn to make people feel a subconscious urge, particularly girls, to lean towards you, simply by leaning back.

This little trick will change your conversations' entire dynamic, giving you the control of a badass. This also means that when you're walking or just standing, you will have your shoulders up and back and your chin up. Just a masculine, healthy posture.

This also suggests that you can have your head up and back and your chin up while you're walking or just standing. Only a balanced and masculine stance.

Look at this image: who is perceived as the individual with the highest status here?

He's happy, Berlusconi is lying back, and his legs are crossed.

Obama bends forward, his hands locked, and so are his legs.

Think of it this way, leaning forward or backward communicates two opposite sentiments. Leaning forward is a sign of interest—maybe too much of it.

When you're too interested in others, it sends the signal that you don't find yourself interesting enough, that you're following rather than leading, or like in this picture, you accede that the other person is superior to you.

Leaning backward sends different messages to a woman and other people about how you feel about yourself and others. One is that you're of course, confident. Only people who are truly relaxed can afford to lean back and hold that position long enough.

Those who aren't confident will find this to be a very awkward position and after a minute or two, they'll revert to their original and consistent omega male, low-status posture.

Second, leaning back sends the message that you're not that interested in the hot chick you're with or eyeing. Believe it or not, this can pose a very big challenge for hot women who are used to being pursued, hounded and served by omega men.

They're used to "controlling" men that when they find you're not that interested and aren't willing to interact on her terms of dominance, they'll sense deep inside that you're no ordinary man—you're alpha! And when that happens, consider her leaving the front door to her pants open for you!

Lastly, leaning back tells the world that you sincerely believe you're worthy to be followed—that they should follow you. That tells a lot about your confidence level and your ability to control yourself and your situation.

So, lean back, relax and enjoy.

6. Lean Against Things Whenever You Can

Have you ever seen a picture of James Dean?

When you're talking next to a wall, lean against it. Just like James Dean did, always remembering that showing your crotch region is important.

Also, having a wall behind you and a room in front of you is a high-status position. You're in control of the situation in front of you and, subconsciously, you will be recognized as the leader of your group.

Leaning against a wall also sends the message that you're relaxed, calm and collected. These further imply that things are going according to your plans and that you're in control of yourself and your situations. And you know what that means, Dawg. If you don't, then here it is you're subtly telling a woman that you're so in control that she can't order you around and that she's going to have to play by your own rules.

That should make you stand out in her mind as not being an ordinary mortal but that you're different from all the other wimpy omega males surrounding her and vying for her attention. And that should also open her front door into her pants later on.

How to Show Yourself to Others

We've all heard it: in order to genuinely enjoy others, you need to first learn just how to enjoy on your own. And it's true. Unless you reveal unconditional love on your own, you will not permit others to absolutely like you either. The challenge is that these days, our way of living is exceptionally focused on success, contrasting ourselves to others and a desire to do more continually. The result? We have become our very own most significant critics—concentrating on our mistakes as well as where we "might've done better" more than on our successes. So, when we hear that real love hinges on very first loving ourselves, we ask ourselves how in the world we're supposed to move from consistent self-criticism to genuine love.

1. What You Need to Recognize Initially

If there is only one lesson you learned this whole year, it's this: You are the most crucial person in your entire world. Your whole life is lived through your eyes. Your communications with the world and those around you, your thoughts and also how you analyze events, relationships, activities, and also words. You may simply be an additional individual when it involves the grand plan of things, and however, when it means your understanding of truth, you are the only thing that matters. As well as because of that, your truth depends upon just how much you love and also look after yourself.

Your connection with yourself is one of the most important things to forming the kind of life you live. The less you enjoy yourself, pay attention to yourself, and also understand yourself, the much more confused, angry, and even annoying your statement will undoubtedly be. However, when you start and also continue to love yourself much more, a lot more, whatever you see, everything you do, as well as everyone you engage with, starts to come to be a little bit better in every way possible.

Yet, self-love isn't pure. As they claim: you are your very own greatest doubter. We're configured to have bouts of self-loathing, and also for a lot of us, these stages of self-hatred can turn into our whole lives. It's when we invest more time disliking ourselves than we do care for ourselves that we embrace an even more unfavorable disposition of the world. To begin to love yourself initially might not be the most useful thing on the planet to do, however, it's undoubtedly the most essential.

2. Your Daily You

Consider individuals in your life that you love and also regard. Just how do you treat them?

You respect them, patient with their thoughts and suggestions, and also forgive them when they make a mistake. You provide space, time, and opportunity; you make sure they have the room to grow since you love them sufficient to rely on the potential of their growth. Currently, think of exactly how you treat yourself. Do you provide yourself with love and also regard that you might offer your closest pals or better half?

Do you care for your body, your mind, and your needs?

Below are signs that you could be showing your mind and body self-love in your day-to-day life:

- Sleeping properly
- Eating healthy and balanced
- Providing yourself time and also room to recognize your spirituality
- Exercising frequently
- Thanking yourself and those around you
- Playing when you require it
- Staying clear of vices as well as hazardous impacts
- Showing and also practicing meditation

How many of these everyday activities do you enable on your own? As well as if not, then exactly how can you claim you enjoy yourself?

Loving yourself is more significant than merely a state of mind—it's additionally a collection of activities as well as routines that you embed right into your day-to-day life.

You have to reveal to yourself that you love yourself, from the get-go of your day to the end. I understand that saying it is better than doing it. However, the primary method I recommend is offering yourself time and room to exercise meditation methods. I made use of to be deeply dissatisfied, but I altered my life by getting stuck into the Buddhist viewpoint as well as adopting some fantastic reflection techniques.

This is effective as well as the practical method you can find out to like on your own. Not only that, but via reflection, you'll improve your focus, lower your tension and also be familiar with yourself on an intimate level. Via meditation and also mindfulness techniques that I utilize every day, I have learned to approve myself just as that I am; it is a vital component of caring for yourself. It's complicated, and it will undoubtedly take effort. Yet, if you stick at it daily, you'll eventually experience the benefits that so many individuals talk about with meditation.

3. Accepting the Discomfort

Nobody is excellent. A few of us confuse self-love with limitless positivity and countless optimism. Some tackle their day singing the commends of God no matter exactly how poor they may be feeling or just how terrible their predicament may be. And we believe this is the good thing to do; besides, shouldn't positive vibes merely draw in even more positive vibes?

But the reality is that your many positive outlooks are a massive lie. You're lying to a part of yourself, overlooking the demands of half of what you are. Because most of us have a dark side; we all hold distress, disgust, and pain. Disregarding these realities consumes us up, as well as compels us to cave-in spiritually and also emotionally. Enable yourself to be sincere with who you are. Forgive yourself for your past actions, those points you are ashamed of. Accept that you are occasionally a service provider of adverse feelings, like disgust, rage, and envy. And also find out to embrace the silence when you require it.

4. Discover and also Open Your Heart

While step 3 has to do with recognizing and also approving the discomfort, step 4 is about resolving with a relaxed and unopened heart. Passing your defects and your faults is one point, but enjoying a person that can have your thoughts, your feelings, your vices, as well as your blunders? That's an altogether higher degree of vanity.

Discover your life story. Trace your course from childhood years to the individual you are currently. Understand yourself in the most intimate means feasible, and find the reason for every single negative emotion, every shameful act, every word, and also deed, that you now are sorry for. Take the skeletons out of your wardrobe as well as attempt to keep in mind why they are there in the first place.

Probably the most critical point you will uncover is that most parts of our character have a cause, as well as those that can't be learned away. Possibly you have false understandings of truth, or trauma, or feelings of victimhood. Probably you see the world in a different way than it is, and also due to that, you made points you currently known to be wrong.

Find the reasons and map your past. Learn to enjoy yourself in a way that just you can. Quit repenting of your past and also begin understanding it. When you hide away old feelings, you put yourself in a cage of your own making. The only escape is to push with the unpleasant facts you've been repressing. If you go near the side of the cage, you feel extreme pain. Because of the location of pain, you can ultimately take care of past injury as well as discomfort.

Mindfulness is vital to leave your mental cage. The more you take care of past emotions through mindfulness, the less psychological disturbance can happen. Emotional disruption is based on something that occurred to you long ago, something you have not let go of.

If mindfulness has a lot of evident advantages, why doesn't everyone do it?

Right, here's what I believe. A great deal of details concerning mindfulness is massive as well as challenging to comprehend. For instance, advice about thanking deep space or experiencing happiness simply isn't appropriate to many people's lives. And I believe mindfulness—a functional, realistic technique that every person can exercise—has been lumped with new-age nonsense like "the law of destination," "power" and "vibrations," These expressions might seem reasonable. However, they do not operate in truth.

5. Share Yourself

On this path of self-discovery, you will undoubtedly uncover truths about yourself that will horrify and also stun you. However, the objective is to function your way through them and begin to enjoy yourself more with understanding as well as approval. And also, only after you have worked out your bumps, can you start to see the rough diamonds: your gifts. These are the qualities regarding you that survive the journey. The compassion, the spirituality, the humor, the love: every little thing you have cleaned off after cleaning away all the remainder. And when you enjoy on your own and also the things concerning you, just then can you effectively share yourself to the globe. Offer your true self to the world as well as those around you. Since you like yourself, it's time to start assisting others in locating the highest kind of self-love of their very own.

6. Your Ideas Are Simply Thoughts—Nothing More

The key thing you should realize is that most of us are naturally adverse. We have thousands of concerning ideas every day, and amazingly, 70 percent of them might be harmful. Because worries and fears are needed for us to protect ourselves. Yet this survival mechanism can work against us, which is why you're experiencing insecurity and also self-criticism now.

So, what can you do?

Well, what you need to understand is that while your opinions can not always be changed, you can stop believing them. Ideas are just thoughts—nothing more. Below is an inspiring quote from Allan Lokos:

"Don't think everything you assume. Thoughts are simply that—ideas."

7. Accept Your Emotions Without Evaluating Them

Whenever we experience an unpleasant feeling, such as despair, fear or rage, our initial reaction is to ignore it, deny it or press it away. And this is reasonable enough, we don't wish to walk feeling psychological pain regularly. Nonetheless, when we decline our emotions, we might make facts worse.

Feelings give us valuable information concerning our lives. A far better strategy that might assist your emotional wellness is to exercise acceptance. This suggests stopping negatively judging your emotions or just trying to change them. It's comprehending that you don't need to "regulate" your feelings. They can refrain from any type of damage to you.

The essential things you do to do away with negative emotions, like alcohol or eating cake, can do more damages to you. Learning to accept your feelings might cause steady emotional durability. Nonetheless, it is essential to not confuse acceptance with self-imposed suffering. When you are dealt with unfairly by a superior, that doesn't indicate you should approve it. Acceptance is about balance. Western society encourages us to be favorable regularly. However, that's not reasonable. Instead, we have to live our lives with both the bad and also the good, which helps us live a life of happiness. In the end, if you can approve yourself and all of your feelings, you'll be a lot more conveniently able to enjoy on your own.

PART III.

Body Language and Culture

ELLEN LEWIS

Cultural Differences in Body Language

History tells us that people started to shake hands to convey peaceful intentions to others (and also the fact that they did not hide any weapons). Today, the handshake has become a common greeting ritual, helping one demonstrate the present level of confidence. A handshake can provide a lot of information regarding the person in question, especially when it comes to how willing he/she is to allow someone else in his/her personal space.

Handshakes can either be too weak or too strong, each situation conveying a different message about the person shaking those hands. If the handshake is too weak, this means that the person in question is not confident enough, being anxious or nervous with regard to the current interaction. A handshake that is too strong can mean a desire to dominate or over-confidence.

Cultural differences influence the meaning of handshakes as well. For example, in European countries, it is customary for men and women to shake hands, either as a greeting or as a form of agreement for a certain decision. In Muslim countries, such an interaction is forbidden and severely frowned upon. We return to the issue of cultural sensitivity once more. We must always pay attention to culture and decide in an instant whether a certain gesture is culturally acceptable or not.

In countries like India, there does not seem to be much of a requirement to maintain a personal distance. It is pretty common to stay at a close distance when communicating with someone; whether you are with a stranger or not. China is another country in the world where people are not very much concerned about personal distance when interacting. The personal distance they keep is less important than accomplishing the goal of the conversation and interaction.

The precedent of keeping a safe personal distance is also very common and widespread in the western world. Did you know that personal space also entails some touching? Yes, that is the case and it's taken very seriously in South American and Mediterranean cultures. In these cultures, the general belief is that a conversation can be enhanced if one person in the conversation touches another. Their connection will also be stronger. Those who don't touch their friends while conversing are taken to be cold-blooded. Over in the eastern world, touching a person as you talk is largely a taboo, and doing such a thing is taken as an offense. Actions like patting somebody in the back or even on their arms are unacceptable.

It is proposed that you study more about body language in that culture and what is considered acceptable, particularly for personal distance, before traveling to such countries. Inappropriate body language may lead to you becoming perceived as a bad-mannered person once you do things to someone from that culture or background. Whether it is more appropriate to stay closer or farther away, make sure to educate yourself on which distance is the most suitable for the culture of the people you will be communicating with. Personal distance is one of the most important aspects of body language and carries a lot of implications in non-verbal communication. Another important part of body language and communicating with people from different cultures is your handshake.

Looking Down VS Chinese Culture

We've all heard the old saying about how it's better to look up. But what does this really mean? Is that true for every culture?

In Chinese culture, looking up is a gesture of respect and awe. Consider the Olympic torch relay - it trails off as runners bow to each other while passing by. The flame symbolizes integrity, honesty, high ideals, wisdom and intelligence - all qualities one should aspire to have in order to ascend higher on the social ladder in China.

Legs Apart VS Chinese Culture

This is a predominantly male stance that indicates a stable, unmovable posture and mindset. This stance is indicative of an assertion of dominance and says that this person is standing their ground and maintaining their point of view.

There are a diversity of enlightenments why this is mostly a male viewpoint. There are cultural customs such as the ancient Chinese custom where a woman's feet were bound to indicate her dependence on her husband. The woman's feet were bound so tightly that they were unable to stand without pain being caused.

Apart from the possible cultural reasons where this can be seen as a predominantly masculine pose, the fact that men are generally taller makes it easier for them to adopt this pose and assert dominance. Their height makes it easier to also showcase their genital region as a sign of vitality. This is why women generally see men who adopt this pose as more attractive. This pose is also a signal to other men that this man is dominant in his environment. A typical example of where this can be seen is at sports events where men stand tall with their heads high, chest puffed out and groin region highlighted.

As a side note, if you feel down or not confident on the way forward, take a few moments to adopt this pose with your head held high and your shoulders held back. This is a power pose, and this physical manifestation of power is likely to make you feel mentally and emotionally more powerful, in control, and more capable of handling the problems that arise in your life. Saying a few firm positive affirmations, which are statements that manifest positivity into your life, enhances this effect.

Whether man or woman, this is a stance that is normally taken up by people who are predominantly assertive in nature and communication behavior. Verbally, such a person typically speaks in a clear tone of voice and is not afraid to voice their opinion.

Crossed Leg Position VS Middle Eastern and Asian Culture

Crossing the legs while standing is typically a sign of submission or defensiveness. It signifies denied access to the genitals and is considered a closed posture. It is normally seen in settings where the people there are not familiar with one another and thus, are unsure how to interact with each other. In relation to whether the members of that conversation were relaxed with each other, it is typically followed by a guarded face and crossed arms together with a greater physical distance. This closed stance is indicative that the person is emotionally withdrawn from the conversation.

This is a sharp contrast to the more open uncrossed pose when standing. This pose indicates openness or dominance as it presents the genitals.

A person can move from a closed to an open posture as they begin to gain comfort in the setting or communication process. There are typically a series of moves that show that person is letting their guard down and becoming less defensive. Of course, that process begins with the closed position of legs and arms closed but as they relax, the first sign of this is typically the uncrossing of the legs so that the feet are placed in a parallel stance. Next, the arms typically are uncrossed, and hand gestures come into play. Taking a foot forward stance comes next to show acceptance of the communication process and the other person. It shows emotional investment in the conversation.

While sitting, a person can also cross their legs. When approximately 70 percent of the global population sits, they cross the left leg over the right. Emotional detachment from the contact process was also commonly suggested.

A person may also sit in a 4-cross leg position. This person will normally lean forward. This stance is indicative of an argumentative or competitive stance and is a normal form of behavior from aggressive or assertive communication behavior. It's meant to convey that an individual is relaxed, assertive and youthful. You need to be careful with this stance, though, depending on whom you are communicating with as it can be seen as insulting in Middle Eastern and Asian cultures as showing the sole of one is associated with dirt and filth.

Adopting a legs clamp posture, which is where a person adopts a 4-cross leg position, but places one or both hands on their legs to form a clamp is seen as entirely aggressive body language. It is a sign that a person is stubborn and refuses to accept the opinion of other people.

Locking the ankles rather than crossing the legs is seen as a sign that a person is holding back information. This can be seen as a sign of lying or deceit in men. However, when it comes to women, locking their legs at the ankles is a matter of practicality depending on what the woman is wearing. While wearing a skirt, this is a common pose that women adopt to protect certain parts of their body from public eyes.

Hand Talking VS Italian and French Culture

Because the hands are such a powerful tool used in communication, a raised hand has been seen as a sign of authority or power over others for thousands of years. This gesture was so significant that all the persons of power or authority had to do was simply raise their hand to signal that they had the floor and so, no one else was allowed to speak or interrupt during that time. This gesture dates back so far that persons of lower social status were executed for interrupting Julius Caesar in Roman history.

We live in a vastly different time and era now, but the raised hand still holds significance when used in social settings. Just look at the Italian and French cultures and you will notice that they are two societies that still place great significance on hand talking. In the Italian culture, taking a turn to talk in a group setting (even a group of just two) is a simple matter of raising your hand to signal that you want the floor. As a sign of respect to the talker, listeners will place their hands down or behind their back to show that they have recognized the symbol and are granting this person's request to hold the floor at that particular time.

The only trick is to get your hand up as fast as possible when you would like the floor to get a word in. Don't worry, this is not that difficult. It is a simple matter of looking away or touching another person's arm to show that you would like a turn to have the floor. The Italian culture is one where there is a lot of physical touch and outsiders might see this as being overly friendly and intimate but in actuality, Italians use such touching because they place great significance on these gestures to send messages in communication. They are smartly trying to restrict the gestures of each other's hands so that they can take the floor. In fact, they usually reserve the right hand for demanding that attention while articulating their points and showcasing their emotions with the left hand. Therefore, right-handed people have an upper hand in conversation in this culture. Pun intended!

Offending Signals Around the World

L anguage, one would say, is of the most inquisitive human innovations; however, what would you be able to say about motions? Truly, body language has its own peculiarities, history, and even geological dispersion. What may appear as though an innocuous joke in one part of the world can be very offending in the other.

The Middle Finger

An exemplary in Western culture, the middle finger advises somebody to leave. Different equivalents for this motion are "giving somebody the flying creature," "giving somebody the finger," or "flipping somebody off." You will be surprised to find that in Ancient Greece it has its causes and was used in Ancient Rome at that point in a hostile way because it looks very much like male genitals. From then on, it has become an image of resistance, refusal and discontent.

The Approval

Thoughtlessly offering somebody a go-ahead in Greece, Iran, Russia, Sardinia and parts of West Africa could get you in a tough situation! There, an approval is inseparable from giving somebody the middle finger. Notwithstanding, this is one of the most flexible signs the world over. In many nations, it's an indication of endorsement and satisfaction, while in others, the thumb is utilized as a portrayal of the number 1 when tallying or even for bumming a ride!

The A-Okay

You may believe you're indicating your gratitude or acting like an expert scuba jumper utilizing this sign, yet it's sharp to peruse the room first. You could coincidentally blame somebody for being a disappointment (in middle and southern Europe, for example, since the image could be deciphered as "zero") or even representing a horrendous aspect of the body while assaulting the other person's sexuality (in Brazil, Turkey and Venezuela).

The Fig

Playing "got your nose!" with a youngster? Ensure you're not doing it in Turkey, Greece, Indonesia, Madagascar, and Slavic nations. This motion is annoying because it represents a sexual demonstration. It's thought to have originated in ancient Indian culture and has been used to keep bad luck away from the family since Ancient Rome!

The Arm of Honor

This "arm of honor" is notable in Romance-speaking Europe, Latin America, Russia, Poland, Hungary, Bulgaria, Croatia, Turkey, Georgia, Québec, Ireland, and parts of Scotland. If you haven't seen it before, know that it's identical to the middle finger. The great part? You're not going to do it inadvertently since it takes two arms and some coordination to complete it!

The Horns

In Portugal, Spain, France, Italy, Greece, Mexico, and Brazil, just as the Baltics, you're shrewd to stay away from this motion, particularly if you point it at somebody! By utilizing it, you're telling that person that their partner is undermining them and that everybody knows, along these lines affronting their partner. Is doing it at a stage performance hostile? The appropriate response is no! Individuals do it in any case because the setting is everything.

The Moutza

Have you ever given somebody "the hand" when they're looking at something you couldn't care less about? It's fundamentally the same signal as the most conventional affront in Greece. In addition to the fact that it signifies that you'll spread the other person's face with ash, it can likewise be magnified by playing out a twofold moutza utilizing two hands covering each other.

The Forks

The English-speaking world has given us an innovative contort on the gesture of goodwill called "the forks" or "two-fingered salute." It's a hostile signal in Australia, the United Kingdom, South Africa, New Zealand, India, Pakistan, and Ireland. It's equivalent to giving somebody the middle finger. Thought to have had its starting points in fifteenth-century England, the offending V sign stays an indication of insubordination, notwithstanding authority and scorn.

The Failure Sign

The state of an L on your brow implies you're calling somebody else a loser. Famous in the United States during the 1990s because of two or three films (to be specific, Ace Ventura: Pet Detective and The Sandlot) and the tune "All-Star" by Smash Mouth (1999), it appears to be genuinely guiltless, however, realize that it's an insult if it's aimed at you! You're probably going to discover this motion in mainstream society.

Pointing at Somebody

Indeed, numerous societies around the globe think of it as impolite to point at somebody. A few nations, in any case, pay attention to it more than others. In Cambodia and Malaysia, pointing with your index is considered incredibly impolite. Individuals either take a stab at pointing with two fingers, with their thumbs or with the entire hand.

Calling Somebody by Twisting Your Finger

This may appear to be fun-loving in Europe and North America, however, do likewise in the Philippines, and you may see some furious countenances. Twisting the forefinger is utilized to call canines, as it were. This implies doing likewise for people is very disparaging and hostile. If you're attempting to call somebody, utilize your whole hand or arm to make your aim known.

Fingers Crossed

Crossed fingers may be one of the most unpredictable motions designed by humankind. It can mean you're lying (particularly if you cross your fingers despite your good faith). In different settings, it can mean you're pulling for somebody to be effective (consequently the articulation "Fingers crossed!"). However, in Vietnam, it implies something different altogether: you're offending somebody by recreating female privates, not wishing them karma.

Receiving Gifts with One Hand/Your Left Hand

While accepting a gift in China, South Korea, Japan, and Vietnam use two hands to get it. This shows you completely put resources into the second and care about the other person's nice thoughts. If you utilize just one hand, that may be seen as indiscreet, discourteous, or entitled. In India and the Middle East, ensure you utilize either two hands or your right hand only, as the left hand is normally observed as the messy one.

Touching Somebody's Head

Touching a head is hazardous anyplace. Ensure you keep away from it, particularly in nations with enormous Buddhist populaces like Cambodia, China, Laos, and Thailand. These societies see the head as the holiest aspect of our bodies. Sightseers neglect to consider that contacting sculptures' heads is similarly hostile, so check your posture before your next touristy picture!

The "You Have Five Dads"

One of the most intricate hostile signals is given to us by the Middle East, including two hands and a considerable amount of exhibition. If you'd prefer to irritate somebody's mom by suggesting she's had a great time with a few men before, this is your go-to sign, yet it's better if you don't! If things go south, this signal could get you expelled or even worse, particularly if you do it in Saudi Arabia. The beneficial thing is that it isn't so natural to do it coincidentally!

PART IV.

Improve Your Body Language

10-Day Challenge

Day 1/10: If You Want to Feel Confident

If you want to feel confident, you have to be decisive. Start making smarter decisions and stop making excuses. You'll start to be more aware of your personality and the way you interact with the world, and it's incredibly satisfying. If you want to start making better decisions, practice saying "Yes" more often. If you're considering checking your email while out with friends, just say "No." If you're having a tough time deciding on what project to work on, just pick one and start working.

Day 2/10: To Make People Participate, Look Like You Are Actually Listening

Great listeners are a rare find. People often feel like they're being listened to only when they're talking. That's why it's so important to look like you're listening, and not looking down with a smartphone in your lap! You'll be surprised at how much more willing people are to talk to you, and what kind of strangers will jump out of the woodwork to tell you their life stories.

Day 3/10: Shake Hands to Trigger a Connection

Shaking hands is a good way to trigger the mirror neurons in your brain, and forge a connection with other people. It creates an instant sense of empathy that can carry on throughout the day. People tend to like each other more when they talk for longer. You can easily keep someone talking by asking them questions, and letting them monologue in response. Ask about their background, what they do for fun, where they're from, etc..

Day 4 /10: Smile to Promote Good Feelings

A smile has a miraculous power to alter the way you feel. When you smile, you automatically feel happier. Even if it's forced, your brain will treat it as genuine and release more endorphins, which translate to good feelings! You can make every interaction a little bit better by smiling. Smile at cashiers and say "thank you." Smile at the barista when ordering coffee or a snack. Smile at your friends, family, and colleagues. You'll notice a vast variance in the way you feel, and the way other people treat you.

Day 5/10: Encourage Collaboration by Removing Barriers

Collaborating is a good way for everyone to learn and grow. You'll solve problems more quickly, help others, and learn from their experiences. When you collaborate with other people on a project, you'll naturally share ideas to improve each other's ideas. You'll enjoy working with a team of people who are as passionate about the project as you are. Collaboration breeds positivity and happy feelings to everyone involved.

Day 6/10: Improve Your Speech with Your Hands

When you're presenting or talking in front of a group, don't just speak with your mouth. Use your hands to get everyone's attention, and to help them follow along. Use gestures and show the audience what you're talking about. You'll feel more confident when you're speaking, and people will remember what you just said much more easily!

Day 7/10: Look at People's Feet for Added Insight

People tend to focus on your face when they're talking to you. However, you can use your height and the way that you stand to your advantage. Look at people's feet when they talk to you, and adjust yourself accordingly. It's a subtle thing, but it will help you feel more confident and look like a leader to your team members.

Day 8/10: Keep Your Voice Low for an Authoritative Sound

When speaking to somebody who is older than you, keep your voice lower, and speak slower. It will give you an authority figure sound that they'll respect. You can use the same technique when speaking to children! Lower your voice on their level, and speak very slowly. It will make you feel more confident when speaking to people of all ages!

Day 9/10: How to Be a Good Boss

The following are some tips on how to be an effective and respected boss. Some of them relate to body language but most amount to common decency and consideration:

- Motivate by positive rewards and incentives, not fear of punishment.

- Praise your workers in public and criticize them in private only.

- Offer credit where credit is due; never take credit for others' accomplishments.

- Gain the respect of employees by taking a personal interest in them and their problems.

- Once you have delegated a task to an employee allow them to do it in their own way.

- Make it clear that if they have an issue to discuss, "your door is always open."

- Be a good listener. Let them know your priorities, but be open to their ideas on how they can excel in a project. As far as possible, let them settle disputes with other staff themselves without intervening in favor of one or the other.

- Be tolerant and understanding of personal problems that may arise and allow some leeway regarding time off when a life crisis has occurred.

- Keep it light. Try to maintain a sense of fun in the workplace so that your staff is happy to come to work.

Day 1/10: How to Deal with a Bad Boss

- Try to agree with them as much as possible without compromising your own values and efficiency. This makes it easier to disagree when it is absolutely necessary.

- Be able to admit that you might be wrong occasionally. Don't always try to show that you are brighter or stronger.

- Don't ask your colleagues to side with you against the boss—ultimately, they may sacrifice you for their own advancement.

- If you believe that you are being threatened or intimidated, try to avoid playing the race/gender card. Document details of exactly what was said and done, where and when, and send a memo to the boss outlining why you think the behavior inappropriate.

- If matters are not resolved, update your CV and consider looking for another job. Redress through industrial tribunals leaves a bitter taste and may backfire to your long-term detriment.

Conclusion

In this book, we have learned that we use Body Language every day. In our fast-paced world, human interactions are often rushed. We rush in and out of important meetings, rush to catch the train or rush through work. To ensure a harmonious interaction with others, we use body language subconsciously. While we may feel that we are acting in a friendly manner, we in fact say things like "yes," smile, and shake hands. Our body language speaks volumes.

Needless to say, as children, we were trained to use all of these techniques. It was deemed appropriate for us to use these body language techniques to help us to be better people.

We often convey our feelings by the movement of our hands or body. When we are feeling happy, we clap our hands. When we are feeling sad, we cross our arms in front of us and avoid eye contact. When we are frustrated, we shake our heads slowly from side to side.

In addition to these gestures, handshaking is more than just a gesture of greeting. The handshake can indicate whether someone is trustworthy or not. A firm handshake conveys strength and confidence, while a limp handshake can indicate weakness and lack of ability. Smiling and laughter can ensure successful interaction with others.

It is deceptively simple to take a person's hand and help them find their true purpose in life. Learning to communicate with others, however, can be a lifetime process. Communication is not the same as understanding people. Understanding people comes after you have communicated with them.

Non-verbal communication is important in our everyday lives. It is the way we communicate with others without saying a word. We can manipulate our feelings by moving or arranging our bodies. Body language can help diagnose our emotional states. It can help individuals in all paths of life communicate effectively and strengthen social bonds between people.

Most of our communication is non-verbal however, most people do not take the time to look at their body language. It reveals how we feel, what we are thinking and how others perceive us even before we speak a word.

This book taught us that we are responsible for how we are seen since we are in control of our bodies. It produces healthier relationships in our lives when we decide to give meaningful messages to other individuals based on deep feelings. It also shows us the value of being human and understanding at the deepest levels of our existence. Human beings are in charge of their actions. It's fair to say we're building the way we want people to see us.

Still, always remember: You only have control over your own values, actions, and reactions. You cannot make people like you if their values are different from yours. So, instead of gazing outward, turn your eyes inward. Start becoming a better version of yourself!

Introduction

The human brain maybe manipulated and controlled through the art and science of dark psychology. Dark psychology is psychological science and the art of mind control and manipulation. Every individual has a dark side in them, but the problem lies in how you can manipulate it. Once you have successfully tapped into the dark side of a human being, you will not be able to control them. Things will start to happen in their lives as per your commands; even they will not be able to understand how all this is happening. All they know is that everything is going right with their lives for no apparent reason.

This book will enlighten you to the manipulative tacticsthat manipulators employ to gain control over. Discover the techniques that make master manipulators!

To the uninitiated, master manipulators are mysterious characters. They are seen as powerful magicians and experts at deception. The truth is that master manipulators use no intricate craft to deceive and influence others. Instead, they use a combination of small but powerful techniques to get what they want. They use everything from subliminal messages to body language to make people believe what they want them to believe. This book reveals the secrets of manipulation in the everyday life. It gives the tools you need to see through the distractions that come from being manipulated and helps you regain control over your mind and your actions.

Emotions are extremely complex. Maintaining your composure in any situation is a difficult task. There are many ways to distract, confuse, and manipulate others. Learn the secrets of body language, deception, manipulation, and subliminal messaging.

Most people see these dark tactics as negative, but the truth is that many dishonest people have been successful in doing this with ease. However, you can never know your abilities until you can see them and learn how they influence your behavior.

The truth is every individual is capable of being manipulative. While most individuals are aware of using these dark tactics, others use them without even knowing. The problem of being manipulative, psychologically, is that it can interfere in the development of the people around you. With that said, one needs to be aware of the manipulation tactics, and then, learn and practice alternative ways of being.

There are many forms of manipulation although some are slightly subtler than others. For instance, consider the case of a boss who is unhappy with his secretary's work performance. He may scold her quite harshly when she comes into work that day but later, he may reward her by allowing her to work at home after hours because he truly admires her hard work ethic, but this will only make her more eager to please him in the future so she will always receive rewards for doing good work for him even though she doesn't necessarily deserve it. Admit it or not everyone needs to feel a sense of belonging such as belonging to a family or community or religion, etc...

Learn the simplest way to detect deception. Emotions can be faked to the point that you may not even realize you are being tricked. Discover and open your eyes how some bow to the will of others.

PART I.

Recognizing the Problem

What Is Emotional Manipulation?

Now that we have enclosed the basic foundations of dark psychology, including the concept of seriously dangerous psychopathy and the irreversible movement toward the Dark Singularity, you may feel a sense of relief that these social problems have been identified and that a system for addressing them has been established.

However, the truth of dark psychology is that lower levels of these deviant personality traits are extremely common. Worse yet, they are often legitimized by the very institutions and people we depend upon to address such violations. Especially in the contemporary environment, in which technology has fostered and encouraged the development of alienation and anti-social lifestyles to the unprecedented degree that they now provide a potentially viable and sustainable means of financial and social support, understanding how dark psychology manifests itself can make the difference between success and failure. As the following diagram illustrates, your ability to establish a high level of emotional intelligence has a direct effect on your job performance:

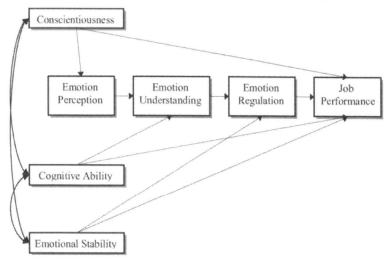

Effect of emotional intelligence on job performance, n.d.

Types of Emotional Manipulation

Discussing manipulative behavior accurately requires that we examine this problem from 2 perspectives: from the perspective of clinical psychology and the perspective of everyday relationships. We will begin by discussing diverse types of emotional manipulation using clinical terminology.

Characteristics of a Manipulative Relationship

First, one theory states that emotional manipulation is essentially a one-sided activity in which all of the effort to create, execute, and sustain a manipulative relationship is made by the manipulator. Such relationships generally have 3 defining characteristics:

Concealment

The true motivations of the manipulator—aggression and control—are concealed by behavior that appears friendly and helpful.

It is more difficult to conceal problems with aggression and control in our personal, intimate relationships, our friendships, and our relationships among family members. As a result, these types of relationships are more likely to develop in the workplace or your community among business owners and their staff or other professionals.

In the less-regulated world outside of the workplace, emotional predators may exploit the trust they have established by making unreasonable demands on your time, asking for favors, and putting pressure on you to agree by suggesting there could be repercussions at work. A truly gifted manipulator will know how to make this threatening behavior look and feel friendly and perfectly reasonable until you have been too badly compromised to take any action to reverse course.

Profiling

The manipulator will have studied the vulnerabilities of the victim so that will be able to exploit them more effectively.

This type of predatory conduct has become much worse in the current environment of surveillance and social networking sites.

Amorality

The manipulator will possess high degrees of amorality and a lack of remorse, both of which enable behavior that is ruthless, cunning, and treacherous.

Often, we expect that a simple, polite request to cease harmful, rude, or disruptive behavior should be sufficient to end predatory or violative misconduct. Although we may be right, Dark Triad personalities (Narcissism, Machiavellianism, and psychopathy. You will see later) who lack empathy find it easy to engage in amoral behavior. Even worse, far from feeling any remorse as a result of committing abuses, they often feel a great sense of joy, victory, and accomplishment. As the saying goes, such reactions add insult to injury.

Categories of Emotionally Manipulative Behavior

Understanding the basic dynamics of manipulative and abusive relationships is important. Each of these general types of relationships may be characterized by specific types of behavior. Psychologists have identified many specific techniques of behavior modification commonly employed by emotional manipulators. Some of these techniques include:

- **Positive reinforcement:** This technique was identified by the behavioral psychologist B.F. Skinner, whose theory of operant conditioning resulted from his experiments with small animals placed in cages. In his experiment to prove the theory of positive reinforcement, he used cages equipped with 2 levers—one lever did nothing, while the other produced a food pellet whenever the small animal pushed it. Soon, the animals learned through positive reinforcement which lever to push to get their reward.

- Emotional manipulators employ positive reinforcement in their strategies by using techniques such as praise, false and superficial demonstrations of emotions such as charm and sympathy, excessive rewards including gifts, money, approval, and attention, and other outward demonstrations of emotion meant to make the victim feel good.

- **Negative reinforcement:** The other part of Skinner's experiment proved the effectiveness of negative reinforcement. For this part of his experiment, small animals were again placed in cages, which were

119

again equipped with 2 levers. This time, the cages were charged with a mild voltage of electricity that caused slight discomfort to the animals that were placed in them. Once inside the cages, the animals would press 1 of the 2 levers. One of the levers did not produce any results, while the other stopped the electrical current, relieving the discomfort. Soon, the animals learned to press the lever that lessened their pain.

- **Intermittent reinforcement:** Intermittent reinforcement can be either positive or negative and is used to create doubt, fear, or uncertainty. An emotional manipulator may "train"the victim by imposing inconsistent reward and punishment mechanisms to lessen the victim's sense of confidence, control, and autonomy.

- For example, in a romantic relationship, the predator may condition the victim to wear certain clothing, listen to certain music, eat certain types of food, and work at a certain type of job. As the victim in this relationship gains confidence, the predator may begin to discourage their victim, who will be caught off guard. As the victim scrambles to respond, the manipulator may again change tactics.

- **Punishment:** Punishment is a very basic form of emotional manipulation that may involve an entire range of psychologically and emotionally negative and damaging behavior, such as threats, yelling, nagging, complaining, intimidation, insults, guilt, and other forms of emotional blackmail. Skilled predators may find a way to incorporate this abusive and controlling behavior into the relationship over time so that the victim will develop a tolerance for abuse.

- **Traumatic one-trial learning:** This technique is related to the use of punishments, but rather than a feature of a long-term relationship, these techniques involve discrete episodes in which the manipulator uses verbal abuse, demonstrations of anger, and other forms of dominance and intimidation to discourage the victim from certain types of behavior.

Specific Types of Emotional Manipulation

Within these major categories of emotional manipulation techniques, psychologists have also identified a wide range of more subtle variations that we all likely encounter daily. These techniques include:

- **Lying:** Dark Triad personalities, particularly psychopaths, are highly skilled at lying and cheating, so often we may not detect their intent until it is too late. Beware of those who have demonstrated a pattern of dishonesty.

- **Lying by omission:** Lying by omission is a little more subtle. The predator may not say anything untrue but may withhold information that is necessary to cause you to fail.

- **Denial:** Often the damage from emotional manipulation is inflicted after the fact. When you confront someone with evidence of their dishonesty and abuse, their refusal to admit wrongdoing can cause even greater psychological harm.

- **Rationalization:** The increase in popular news media has led to the growth of public relations and marketing firms that produce "spin" to deflect criticism in both political and corporate environments. A rationalization is a form of spin, in which a manipulator explains away their abuse.

- **Minimization:** Like rationalization, a minimization is a form of denial in which the predator understates the seriousness of the offense.

- **Selective attention and/or inattention:** Manipulators will pick and choose which parts of an argument or debate should be considered so that only their views are represented.

- **Diversion:** Manipulators often resist giving straight answers to questions, particularly when they are confronted by their victim. Instead, they will divert the conversation to some other topic or change the subject altogether.

- **Evasion:** More serious than a diversion, a manipulative person confronted with their guilt will often completely evade responsibility by using long rambling responses filled with so-called "weasel words," like "most people would say,""according to my sources," or other phrases that falsely legitimize their excuses.

- **Covert intimidation:** Many manipulative people will make implied threats to discourage further inquiries or resolution.

- **Guilt-tripping:** A true form of emotional manipulation, a manipulator will exploit the integrity and conscientiousness of the victim by accusing them of being too selfish, too irresponsible, or not caring enough.

- **Shaming:** Although shaming can be used to bring about social change when large corporations or governments advance abusive or discriminatory policies, manipulators may attempt to intimidate their victims by using sharp criticism, sarcastic comments, or insults to make them feel bad.

- **Blaming the victim:** This tactic has become increasingly common. When a victim accuses a predator of abuse, the predator will attempt to turn it around by creating a scenario in which the victim alone is responsible for the harm that came to them. The predator may also try to accuse the victim of being the aggressor by complaining about the violation.

- **Playing the victim:** Using the opposite tactic of blaming the victim, the predator will lure a conscientious person into a trap by pretending to have been grievously wounded and cultivating feelings of sympathy. The real plan, however, is to take advantage of the caring nature of the conscientious person by toying with their emotions.

- **Playing the servant:** This tactic is common in environments marked by a strict, well-established chain of command, like the military. Predators become skilled at manipulating this system by creating a persona of suffering and nobility, in which their bad actions are justified as duty, obedience, and honor.

- **Seduction:** This technique does not always have to involve sexual conquest or intimacy. Emotional predators may use flattery and charm to convince people to do their bidding, and they often look for people with low self-esteem.

- **Projection:** This term is used in psychotherapy. Predators who use this technique will look for victims to use as scapegoats. When the manipulator does something wrong and is confronted, he or she will "project"their guilt onto the victim to make the victim look like the responsible party.

- **Feigning innocence:** This technique can be used as part of a strategy of denial. Under questioning, the manipulator will "play innocent" by pretending that any violation was unintentional or that they were not the party who committed the violation. A skilled manipulator who lacks morality and empathy can be very successful at planting the seed of doubt.

- **Feigning confusion:** This technique can also be used as part of a strategy of denial. Under questioning, the manipulator will "play dumb" or pretend to be confused about the central point of the conflict or dispute. By creating confusion, the manipulator hopes to damage the confidence of their victim.

- **Peer pressure:** By using claims, whether true or not, that the victim's friends, associates, or "everyone else" is doing something, the manipulator will put pressure on his victim to change their behavior or attitude.

1. What Do Manipulators Want to Obtain?

What Are People's Reasons for Manipulating Others?

Misery Likes Company

A first, simple reason is that they want to see others frustrated or cause a negative reaction from them. Manipulators are dissatisfied with their lives and themselves and "need" to create problems forother people to bring them down.

They feel empowered by it: When feeling uncomfortable and powerless, a person may frequently strive to assert their dominance in other areas to make up for it. They temporarily feel satisfied when they can influence others to do what they want.

A Lack of Importance

People's percepiton that they are not important is another factor in how they negatively manipulate others. They think that if they only ask for what they want, no one will grant their wish since they aren't important enough. In an effort to prevent disappointment, they instead try to make us feel guilty or ashamed for not doing what they want.

They Are "Too Good" for Some Things

Other manipulators simply believe they are too competent to perform particular duties. They can consider other individuals to be inferior to them and so expect that they will perform the duties that they dislike. Laziness or an inflated sense of self may be the cause.

Not Knowing How to Get Things Done

Some negative manipulators don't think that they are capable of gaining what they want, and instead operate under the assumption that they must convince and pressurize others to do their bidding for them.

Selfishly "Helping" Others

Other negative manipulators convince themselves that what they are doing will help people. This is a common idea embraced by people who think that they know better than others what is best for everyone. Due to their beliefs that they have a higher intelligence or ability, they feel satisfied doing this and convince themselves that the people being manipulated are better off for it.

The majority of negative manipulators are not bad people; they are simply misguided, inconsiderate, insensitive, selfish, and often, weak and insecure. Some of them believe that the people they are manipulating are not as valuable as themselves and that their desires and needs are not as important. This mistaken belief is what allows them to continue to act the way they do without considering the feelings of other people.

Motivations and Intention

Although the act of manipulation is not a one-time event, it is likely that manipulators may only have one goal in mind: obtaining something. The scope of what they are trying to obtain may vary from person to person, and the reasons for their motives could vary in complexity as well. In this section we will explore some common motivations and intentions that influential individuals could be driving by.

Throughout the history of humanity, there has always been a struggle on who can rule over whom. This struggle plays out differently from culture to culture but generally involves power and control over money, territory or people (whether you are successful at obtaining it or not).

Manipulation Can Sometimes Start in Childhood.

In some cases, this struggle may begin when the manipulator is a child. These children may grow up believing that manipulation is the way to get ahead in life and teach themselves or be taught new skills in how to be successful at getting what they want.

These early foundations could set the tone for many of their future relationships and cause them to develop an insatiable desire for power and control over others, which in turn will allow them to feel like they are on top of the world.

What Should You Do?

Suppose you consider yourself with somebody who maintains such strategies in a personal or business relationship, wise up. Because if you're long subjected to it, you're going to pay a huge psychological fee. Here are several thought-provoking things.

It Has Nothing to Do With You

Collect evidence for the diagnosis and then obtain external validation not to believe or accuse it. Since you don't.

Do Not Seek an Explanation or a Shift in Behavior

It would be awesome, but you are not going to get it. And, if you do, that's not going to be true. It's going to be anything they do and get what they want next.

Don't Try to Play Your Own Game With Them

They are going to win. They did that a long time back. From infancy, they might have been tailoring their methods, so they're good—really, very good. But let go of the urge to make the game live.

Set Health and Safety Restrictions

Limits and clear edges are crucial, particularly because of family or other factors you have to preserve the relationship. You may need to have guidance from a trustworthy party outside setting boundaries to adhere to them.

Occasionally, the Exit Door Is the Best Strategy

You should learn for better and get proficient assistance in making a verdict and a schedule if you're unsure. Don't let stuff push on for too long as your quality of life, individuality, and potential are being compromised.

Believing Things Will Change

You ought to hold on to that while you try to improve the condition. It is not a simple matter, but it is real. On the other side, life may be decent, fine, and genuinely wonderful. Go for it.

How to Protect Yourself Against Emotional Predators

Though manipulation does not cause any harm or put the subject in any immediate danger, it is designed to deceive and change the attitude, reasoning, and understanding of the intended subject regarding a particular situation or topic, and it is good to protect yourself and your loved ones against it.

Social influence, such as a teenager inducted into a culture or a society to interact with different people either at home or work, is admirable. Any social influence that regards the privilege and right of individuals to decide, without been intimidated, is usually seen as something helpful.

Then again, social influence is despised when people beguile others to maneuver their way against other people's will. The impact can be very destructive and generally looked down upon as very weak.

Behavioral Traits of the Victims

Manipulation predators or dark manipulators use many techniques to control their victims. They are looking for a specific type of person with certain types of personalities.

Those types of personalities that are often prey to manipulators are those with low or no self-esteem, those who are easy to please, those with low or no self-confidence, who have no sense of assertiveness and are very naïve.

Let's explain these personality traits in more detail:

- Those who are naïve find it virtually impossible to accept the fact that particular people in their lives can be cunning, devious, and ruthless. They will constantly deny that they are being victimized.

- Those who have low self-confidence start to doubt themselves and what they are experiencing. They are not assertive and easily get defensive because they don't want to make waves.

- Those who are emotionally dependent have a submissive and dependent personality. When the victim is more emotionally dependent, the manipulator has an easier time exploiting and manipulating them.

- Those who over-intellectualize want to believe the manipulator and try to understand their reason for harming others, especially the victim themselves.

- Studies have indicated that the triad consists of a lot of undesirable behaviors, such as aggressiveness, impulsivity, and sexual opportunism.

When people show signs of these characteristics, they are trying to get away with using others to get what they want. Each one of these personality traits can make life difficult for people, but all of these traits combined can be dangerous to anyone's mental health.

Those who have any one of these personality traits show some of these behaviors: seeking out multiple sex partners, acting out aggressively to get what they want, having high or low self-esteem, and not viewing themselves highly. Most of these traits are shown by men (Whitbourne, 2013).

Knowing more about the dark triad will help you protect yourself from those who wish to manipulate you and use you to their advantage.

Research has been done to analyze the differences between all 3 personality traits within the triad. They have found that all 3 malevolent personalities.

However, psychopathy and Machiavellianism are more related because of their malicious behavior. Those who fall under the narcissist umbrella are very defensive and are surprisingly fragile.

Their arrogance and ego are just a cover for their feelings of inadequacy. Men are prone to psychopathic traits and behavior due to biological factors (testosterone), as well as social norms.

It is significant to note that individuals who have one of these 3 personality disorders are not trustworthy, are selfish, are not straightforward, are not kind, or modest, and do not comply or compromise, which are all qualities that are not good for any type of relationship.

2. Common Methods of Manipulation

We are going to center on some of the most common but effective methods out there. You will find that this discussion is rather detailed and aimed at providing deep insight into how these strategies are effective.

You will find that some of the methods we will get into a very common and rather overt, while others are rather subtle and go unnoticed. Some of these strategies are so delicate that you don't even know they are there, but they are.

Deception Through Lying

Regardless of the manipulator's ultimate objective, lying is almost always their favorite go-to maneuver. It is the foundation of their playbook. Manipulators will often resort to lies to gain any kind of advantage. Pathological liars are those who compulsively lie all the time, even if there is no need to. When the manipulator is deceptive, it's because they realize that the lies go much better than the facts.

There are several deceptions that the manipulator can use to help them achieve their ultimate goals. Firstly, there are flat-out lies. If the victim doesn't know any better, they will fall for the ruse. The deception takes place as the target is simply misled by false information. This is a pretty straightforward issue.

Things change when the manipulator seeks to cleverly disguise lies by wrapping them up in a context in which they may seem accurate but are truly false. The phenomenon known as "fake news" comes to mind. In fake news, the manipulator will present fraudulent information, which is not known to be true, but also not known to be untrue. So, the target cannot distinguish fact from fiction. The manipulators do everything to persuade others that they are sincere, while the information presented seems to be credible. In the end, the victim has no choice but to go along unless they are willing to do their research to determine if the manipulator is truly lying or being truthful.

What makes fake news even more powerful is when the source of information is credible. And while there is always the possibility that they could simply be wrong about the information they are presenting; manipulators always seek to build up as much credibility as they can. That way, victims will take them at face value. When this occurs, manipulators can become quite dangerous.

Manipulators who lie to their targets are usually good at it. It could be challenging for targets to recognize lies when they are presented. By the time the subject realizes the blatant lie, it is usually too late to change it. Monitoring the various character types that excel at deceit and deception is the only method to guarantee that the target completely removes their risk of manipulation. Most of the time, his targets are unaware of the manipulation until it is too late to stop it. The manipulator would lie about anything to get through.

Lying by Omission

The lie is a bit subtler because the manipulator will tell a few things about the truth but will reject some key issues. This may be called "faking out" in some instances. The manipulator may argue that they must borrow money to get gas or food, but they need the money to buy drugs or alcohol. In this example, they are telling the truth about needing the money. What they are leaving out is the real reason why they need the money.

Half-truths are all about mixing lies with the truth. This is why you need to think things through. If you just blurt out lies without actually thinking about them, then you are liable to make a mistake. If you do, then you'll get caught and your cover will be blown.

For this method to be real, you need to mix lies in such a way that they make sense with scrutinized and contrasted truth. They need to be credible and presented in a manner that makes sense to those who will hear them. Often, manipulators add or omit details that are convenient to them. So, the information is true, on the whole, but the details of the truth are twisted to suit your benefit. As the saying goes, "the devil is in the details."

A good means of implementing half-truths is through rumors. Nowadays, social media is a great way of spreading rumors. It is so effective that you don't need to get people to believe it; all you need is to sow a seed of doubt. As long as you can get people to doubt the accuracy of the information, or partially accept its validity, then you have done your job. By the time the affected parties seek to restore their reputations or set the record straight, it will have been too late. That is why you need to strike first and often. That way, the victim will have no choice but to go into crisis mode.

If you fear such an attack on yourself, then you need to hit the manipulator back where it will hurt them. You need to discredit them at all costs. That will sow the seed of doubt on the source of the information and give you a fighting chance to defend yourself.

Denial

A denial is a form of lying as it entails pretending that something happened when it didn't or trying to hide the fact that something didn't happen when it did. A simple form of denial is trying to avoid responsibility for an action. This is common when a person does something inappropriate but wishes to avoid the punishment that is associated with their actions.

When the manipulator appears to be truly sincere in their defense, the confusion created in those around them can ultimately lead to planting the seed of doubt. This is how skillful trial attorneys can convince jurors that their client is not guilty. Please note that we're not saying that the accused is innocent. What we are saying is that the accused is not guilty as the other party was unable to prove the suspect's culpability beyond a reasonable doubt.

Avoidance

This occurs when manipulators don't give straight answers or move the discussion into a different topic utilizing diversion tactics. In a dialog, avoidance occurs by rambling, or otherwise talking endlessly in a meandering fashion. So, their ultimate game is to confuse the target, which makes them question the true version.

When a manipulator changes the topic, it can be gradual and not entirely obvious.

The manipulator takes advantage of the frustration of the other party. The best manipulators have a way of transitioning attention away from their deeds and on to what they want to achieve. So, don't be surprised if you are dealing with a manipulator if they are constantly trying to dodge your questions or conversation.

Over time, the target can find it difficult to determine what is genuine or not since the manipulator can cause them to question all that they know, or think is valid.

Generalizations

These types of statements a very dangerous insofar as they are intended to be direct attacks on one particular person or group of people. Generalizations can be very unfair, especially when they are intended to characterize a group of people in a certain manner. For instance, when you say things such as "all men are…" or "all women are…" you are misrepresenting people in a truly unfair manner. Yet, when attempting to confuse and deceive people, these statements can be quite effective at creating a negative atmosphere. Manipulators love nothing more than to create animosity among people. After all, one of the fundamental tenets of manipulators is "divide and conquer." Blanket statements are great at achieving that.

Playing the Victim

When we act like victims, we manipulate others. We've learned that since we were kids if you wanted your parents to do something for you, you would lock yourself in your room crying, and this behavior certainly attracted their attention; even today a little victimhood will help you achieve this result. Through victimhood, you can make a person do something for you.

This is one of the motives why numerous individuals go into depression and stay in it. The "feeling special in their problem"allows these individuals to attract the attention of others to feel important in their eyes. This is a sneaky way of manipulating others but equally present in many people.

Generate Fear

The news bulletins are a champion in this. The news tends to terrify us because the more scared we are, the more vulnerable we will be and, therefore, more susceptible to manipulation. Through the use of fear, rulers have the opportunity to manage us better and keep us under control. One remedy we all have at our disposal to defend ourselves against this devious technique is not to watch the news every day. By watching the news, we satisfy what is called the need for "security."

The classic example we can say to understand this technique is when a mother educates her child. If she doesn't want her kid to do something, she tells him something on purpose that frightens him; for example: "if you touch the stove you will burn your hand, and then we have to take you to the hospital." In this way, the child will never go near the kitchen!

It is not necessary to shout or make direct threats to intimidate. Manipulators are experts at sowing fear, many times imperceptibly. It is a matter of announcing dangers in the face of certain behavior.

They manipulate you, for example, when they tell you that you "must" act in a certain way. Otherwise, you run the risk of a certain undesirable situation occurring. They are appealing to reason, after all, they are just trying to condition you through fear.

Create Insecurity

One of the most powerful techniques of mind control is to continuously question everything our interlocutor is telling us. For example, if you say to me: "you know that I was able to achieve this result," I could reply by saying "but are you sure that the result you have achieved is thanks to you?" That way, if we question what others are saying to us, and we do it repeatedly, eventually, others will tend to question it!

There are situations where our weaknesses and convictions or self-love are highlighted, and we take advantage of them.

Negative criticism of what we do or say is manipulative mechanisms based on insecurity. It also happens when they try to confuse us by making our mistakes more complex or by making us believe that they know ourselves better than we do.

PART II.

How People Can Manipulate You

3. Dark Psychology Triad (Narcissism, Machiavellianism, Psychopathy)

Think about the Dark triad as the Bermuda Triangle. The traits of all 3 typically overlap and develop personalities that are destructive and toxic, especially when it concerns intimate connections where we drop our guard.

One female was the subject of identity fraud. Her checking account, as well as a bank card, were jeopardized. She was in love with her sweetheart at that time, who lived with her in her house. She was speaking consistently with the FBI and suffered extreme anxiousness and emotional tension. The authorities were unsuccessful in discovering the criminal.

Her fiancé was very helpful in helping to try to find him. He comforted her, periodically bought her gifts, and took care of paying her monthly rent. When ultimately the property manager confronted her about months of unpaid rent, she understood that the crook was her boyfriend, who had been pocketing her rent money. Her denial made it challenging to accept the truth about his callous gaslighting.

What Is the Dark Triad?

This preferred term was created in 2002 by Paulus and Williams. Dark Triad refers to 3 abnormal, negative personality traits: narcissism, psychopathy, and Machiavellianism. The latter 2 share more characteristics than they share with narcissists. The word usually refers to people with "subclinical" symptoms, suggesting that they do not necessarily have a narcissistic personality disorder (NPD) or antisocial personality disorder (ASPD). Machiavellianism emerged out of Machiavelli's approach and is not a psychological health disorder.

Narcissism is identified by the quest for vanity satisfaction, a feeling of grandiosity, dominance, and entitlement.

Machiavellianism is marked by adjustment—a determining, duplicitous, as well as amoral character, concentrated on self-involvement and personal gain.

Psychopathy is identified by callousness, impulsivity, as well as withstanding antisocial as well as vibrant habits.

- **Narcissism:** this word comes from the Greek Myth of Narcissus, a hunter who fell in love with his reflection in a pool of water, and then drowned. Narcissistic individuals can be selfish, arrogant, lacking in empathy, and oversensitive to objection.

- **Machiavellianism:** the word comes from the famous 16th-century Italian political leader and mediator Niccolò Machiavelli. He earned prestige when his 1513 publication, "The Prince," was interpreted as a recommendation of the dark arts of cunning and deception in diplomacy. Qualities related to Machiavellianism include duplicity, manipulation, self-involvement, and an absence of both feeling and morality.

- **Psychopathy:** characteristics connected with psychopathy include the absence of empathy or sorrow, antisocial behavior, and being manipulative and unstable. It is very significant to keep in mind that there is a difference between undesirable traits and being a psychopath, generally linked to criminal violence.

Typical Dark Triad Traits

A recent research study on the dark triad has attempted to assess these 3 trait differences. To varying degrees, all act boldly out of self-interest as well as lack compassion and regret. People scoring high in these traits are proficient at manipulating and deceive others, though their inspirations for doing so and techniques differ. They violate social standards and even ethical values and lie, cheat, scam, steal, and bully. It's believed that some of these traits are related to genetic factors to some degree.

Due to their damaging behavior, Machiavellianism and psychopathy are more intimately associated, but narcissism is defensive and even more vulnerable. It is because a narcissist's grandiosity and pompousness are a façade that hides much deeper sensations of inadequacy. This distinction is linked to the obvious antisocial behavior connected with psychopathy.

All 3 traits (narcissism to a minimal level) had a low correlation to agreeableness, gauged by the Big-5-character test that examines extraversion, neuroticism, agreeableness, conscientiousness, and openness. Agreeableness varies from beauty as well to personal appeal. It involves dependability, unselfishness, straightforwardness, conformity, generosity, and discreetness, which are essential for partnerships.

Machiavellians and psychopaths are lacking in conscientiousness (Why work when you can cheat and take?) Psychopaths have the lowest degree of neuroticism or unfavorable feelings, which makes them the most sinister. Predictably, narcissists were much more open and a lot more extroverted. Studies show narcissists tend to be creative.

Deception

All 3 characteristics do not have honesty and humbleness which include sincerity, loyalty, lack of greed, and justness. A research study of unfaithfulness revealed that all 3 cheat when the risk of getting caught is low. When the threat is high, psychopaths and Machiavellians (when their energy for reasoning is reduced) cheat anyway. Both will deliberately lie. Narcissists have a high degree of self-deception instead of deliberate dishonesty.

Psychosocial Consequences

The relative study analyzed a variety of actions, including hostility (bullying, sadism, aggressiveness, as well as violence), unpredictable way of living (impulsivity, risk-taking, and substance usage), sexual activity (bizarre fantasies, cheating, and sexual harassment), socio-emotional deficits (absence of empathy, reduced emotional intelligence), poor health (anxiety, isolation, and stress), interpersonal issues (prominence, entitlement, and self-aggrandizement), immorality (lack of values, "deadly sins," as well as ethical disengagement, i.e., "requirements don't apply to me"), and antisocial techniques (unfaithfulness, lying).

In these psychosocial problems, the Machiavellians and psychopaths ranked higher, the psychopaths nearly twice as much as the narcissists. The highest possible ratings were among the latter one, with aggression being the highest attribute. Narcissists scored high in the categories of aggressiveness, sexual problems, interpersonal troubles, and antisocial methods. Amongst all 3 characters, most of the top scores were because of psychopathic characteristics. When those were accounted for, narcissism still madeup interpersonal troubles.

Heartlessness

To understand the absence of empathy among the Dark Triad individualsthe research looked at emotion recognition, which is the capacity to have suitable psychological feedback to other's emotions, cognitive empathy, and the capacity to recognize other's feelings. They discovered that all 3 personality types lacked affective empathy but had an unimpaired cognitive understanding. Creepily, all 3 felt positive looking at sad faces and felt negative seeing happy pictures. Narcissists and psychotics additionally felt great seeing angry faces. Psychopaths liked seeing fearful faces.

The study found that individuals that were high on any one of the 3 personality profiles had the lowest active compassion. Narcissists scored the greatest on cognitive empathy. The reality that these people are aloof to other's feelings while keeping the ability to assess other's opinions, enables them to control people while disregarding their feelings purposefully.

The Effect of Dark Triad Characteristics at Work

It's difficult to find anything positive regarding the Dark Triad attribute's effect in the work environment. Someone with such an emotional makeup would display unfavorable habits, such as being hostile, volatile, self-indulgent, and sly, or all of these combined. In his work, which he wrote in 2013, The Dark Side of Personality at Work, Dr. Seth Spain, an assistant teacher at Binghamton

College School of Monitoring in New York City, stated that there was proof of a "relatively robust connection between Machiavellianism and also unethical decision-making in organizations."

A research study by Delroy Paulhus and Kevin Williams, psychologists at the College of British Columbia, suggests that tendencies associated with narcissism, Machiavellianism, and psychopathy often overlap, yet the 3 are different entities. A further research study located the usual connections between them were dishonesty and an absence of humbleness. Research looking at the Dark Triad at work claims that employees with these personality qualities are "toxic." In some instances, these traits lead people to be much more aggressive in work relationships or attempt to influence people or events extra forcefully. However, at least initially, there is proof that narcissists can manipulate people in relatively favorable, desirable methods. A narcissist will frequently make an effort with their appearance and seem to be enchanting and friendly. They may well be conscientious and achievement-oriented, as that will certainly reflect well on them. But, in time, their continuous "me, me, me" propensity might end up being alienating individuals around them.

How Toxic People Choose Their Victims

The Conversational Narcissist

Have you ever been talking with somebody that keeps interjecting you? Or have you been trying to talk with a person who will not let you speak a word? Conversational narcissists love to speak about themselves, or simply hear themselves speaking. They do not ask you any questions, they do not wait for your response, and they won't stop talking. In a relationship, these individuals will undoubtedly end up being wholly self-centered and will never be attentive to your needs.

The Straitjacket

Someone who wants to control everything and everyone around them is known as a straitjacket. They want to control everything you do, say, and even how you think. You know the person I'm talking about; they go ballistic when you disagree with them and will try whatever to persuade you that they are correct and you should follow their advice. This person won't give you any room to breathe in a relationship. Beware, these people will undoubtedly go after your psychological, conversational, and mental liberty until you have nothing left. Get out while you can!

The Psychological Moocher

Likewise, a psychological moocher is known as a "spiritual vampire" because they tend to draw positivity out of you or bleed you mentally dry. In discussions and partnerships, they never see the positive and often tend to bring every person down with them. If you know someone who only has negative things to say whenever you see them, watch out; it may not get better.

The Drama Magnet

Some toxic individuals are magnets for drama. Something is consistently wrong. Always. Almost naturally, once a problem is resolved, an additional one arises. They just want your empathy, sympathy, and assistance—but not your suggestions! You provide help, yet they never seem to want to properly deal with anything. Instead, they grumble and complain. In a partnership, drama magnets act like victims and put themselves in these situations because it makes them feel wanted. Beware, you could one day become part of the dramatization.

The JJ

A JJ is a jealous-judgmental individual. Envious individuals are exceptionally hazardous because they have a lot of self-hate and can't be happy for any individual around them. Their jealousy commonly manifests itself as a judgmental comment. According to them, everyone else is awful, tiresome, or lacking in some way. If a person starts to express jealously regarding other people, watch out, this could be a toxic individual—moreover, you never know how they talk about you behind your back.

The Fibber

It's tiring to have a hazardous liar in your life. Whether they tell a little lie or a significant one, it's impossible to trust a liar in a partnership. Dishonesty drains us; we regularly doubt their words. If your instinct is ringing alarm bells, then look out; leave before you can get lied to.

The Tank

A take crushes everything in its way. A human tank is continuously right, doesn't take anyone else's feelings into account, and also consistently places themselves first. In a relationship, tanks are exceptionally arrogant. They usually assume they are the smartest individual in the room, so they see every conversation and individual as a challenge. They hardly ever see others as equals, and this can be testing when trying to form a caring connection. If you feel your ideas are being run over, or you are not being valued, get out while you still can!

4. Brainwashing

What Is Brainwashing?

Brainwashing is the process of conniving someone to give up beliefs they had in the past to take on new ideas and values. There are countless means this can be done even though not all of them are considered bad. For instance, if you're from an African country and then move to America, you're often forced to change your values and ideals to fit in with the new culture and environment you're in. Many people have misunderstandings of what is brainwashing. Some people have more paranoid ideas about the practice, including mind control devices sponsored by the government, which are thought to be easily turned on as a remote control. On the other hand, some skeptics don't believe brainwashing is possible at all and lying to anyone who claims it has happened. Most of the brainwashing practice will land in the middle of these 2 ideas somewhere.

During brainwashing practice, the subject will be persuaded by a combination of different tactics to change their beliefs about something. During this process, there is not only one approach that can be used, so it can be difficult to put the practice in a clean little box.

Brainwashing is not a new thing for society. These techniques have been used by people for a long time. Those who were prisoners of wars, for example, were often broken down in a historical context before being persuaded to change sides. Some of these most successful cases would turn the inmate into a very fervent convert to the new side. In the beginning, these practices were very new and would often be enforced depending on who was in charge. The brainwashing term has been developed over time and some more techniques have been introduced to make the practice more universal. The techniques have been introduced to make the practice more universal the newer techniques would rely on the psychology field as many of those ideas were used to demonstrate how persuasive people could change their minds.

The brainwashing process is accompanied by many steps. It's not something that's just going to happen to you as you go down the street and talk to someone you've just met. First of all, one of the main requirements that come with successful brainwashing is to keep the subject isolated. If the subject can be around other people and influences, they will learn how to think as an individual and there will be no brainwashing at all.

Once the subject is isolated, they will go through a process of breaking down themselves. They're told all the things they know are wrong and they're made to feel like they're all wrong. The subject will feel like they're bad after months of going through all of this, and the guilt will overwhelm them. Upon reaching this point, the agent will begin to lead them to the desired new system of beliefs and identity. The subject will be led to believe that all of the new choices are their own and therefore sticking is more likely.

For the most part, when someone is just trying to persuade them from a new point of view, those who undergo brainwashing did so. For instance, if you're in an argument with a friend and they're convincing you their ideas make sense, you've been through brainwashing technically. It may not be evil, of course, and you could logically think about it all, but you were still convinced to change the beliefs you had before. It is very rare for someone to undergo true brainwashing where they will be replaced by their entire value system. It will usually occur in the process of coming to a new point of view, irrespective of whether or not the tactics used were forcible.

Techniques Used in Brainwashing

Rarely employed, the procedures mentioned are used for "true brainwashing." Daily, numerous additional forms of indoctrination take place. They may not force you to entirely give up your old identity in favor of a new one, but they do help you change the way you think and perceive the world.

Hypnosis

Sometimes, hypnosis is used to brainwash people. When under hypnosis, a person becomes highly suggestible. This frequently goes under the banner of relaxation or meditation. The hypnotist can make suggestions to the subject while they are under hypnosis in the hopes that they will behave or respond in some way. Many people first learned about hypnosis through theatre performances. It is frequently utilized to enhance health as well. Everyone has a natural desire to fit in with the "Peer Pressure" crowd. This could occur with a particular group, a family, close friends, or the community. By taking advantage of this strong necessity, the peer pressure approach eliminates the subject's skepticism and allows it to release its resistance to new ideas. If done properly, the subject may be more willing to experiment with new things, less shy about new people, and make new friends easier.

Love Bombing

A strong sense of family permeates most people. You were supposedly born into this group, and you have lived there your entire life. You are the expert on this, and those who lost out on such a connection could feel unwanted and alone. Through emotional ties, sharing of feelings, physical contact, and love bombing, the manipulator can foster a sense of family. By creating a family-like bond between the manipulator and the target, it is simpler to exchange the old identity for the new.

Unbending Rules

The manipulator's rules are frequently rigid and unchangeable. The victim finds it challenging to reason independently and will instead spend their time following the manipulator's instructions. This category can include a wide range of regulations, from those governing confusion and regression to those governing the usage of food, medication, and restroom breaks. These guidelines were put in place to completely manage the victim during brainwashing.

Verbal Abuse

Verbal abuse is one of the tactics used in the breakup phase. Often the victim gets desensitized when bombarded constantly with abusive and foul language. Physical abuse can sometimes supplement or replace verbal abuse.

Controlled Approval

The manipulator will work to maintain confusion and vulnerability during the break-up period. One means to do this is by employing controlled approval. The manipulator will punish and recompense similar actions, in turn, making it difficult for the victim to know right.

Rejecting Old Values

The manipulator wants to get the victim to abandon all of his principles. Bullying, physical threats, and other techniques speed up this process. The target will eventually reject the principles and convictions it once upheld and start to adopt the manipulator's new way of life.

Confusing Doctrine

This tactic will encourage the blind acceptance of the new identity while rejecting other logic the victim will possess. To do so, the manipulator is given a complex set of lectures on an unintelligible doctrine. Through this process, the subject will learn to blindly believe what the agent says, whether it concerns the doctrine or a new identity that is being created.

Metacommunication

This tactic is used when the manipulator inserts subliminal messages into the victim. This is done when the agent emphasizes certain words or phrases which are essential to the new identity. The phrases and keywords are implanted into confusing lengthy lectures through which the subject is forced to sit.

No Privacy

Privacy is a privilege that many victims will lose until they have become a new identity. This is not only taken as a way of making guilt and misdeeds more visible to the victim, but it also removes the ability of the subject to assess the things that are said logically. If the subject has privacy, he or she will have time to take the information he or she received in private and may find that he or she is untrue or not up to what he or she already believes. Removing this privacy means that the agent or officer is always around and always leads the victims to a new identity.

Disinhibition

The manipulator encourages the victim to give childlike obedience during this tactic. This facilitates the manipulator's shaping of the subject's mind.

The Change in Diet

Changing the food consumed by the victim is another tactic that creates disorientation while increasing the sensitivity of the subject to emotional excitement. When the manipulator drastically reduces the food that the victim is allowed to consume, the nervous system of the victim is deprived of the nutrients needed to prosper. In this category, drugs may also be added to the mix.

Games

Games are sometimes used to induce greater group dependency. Games will be introduced, and most of them will be a victim to truly obscure rules. In some cases, the victim is not told about the rules and it must be identified, or the rules are constantly changing. This tactic gives the agent more control.

No Questions

The victim is not allowed to ask questions during the brainwashing process. Issues promote individual thinking, which is dangerous for the practice of brainwashing. If no questions are allowed, it helps the agent to accept the new identity automatically from the victim.

Guilt

The victim was told they are bad and all they do is bad. Guilt is a common tactic used by the manipulator to challenge their beliefs and what happens around them. The sins of the former lifestyle of the victim are exaggerated to bring culpability to life and strengthen the need for salvation in the victim. Fear is a powerful motivator and can do much more than the other tactics listed. Manipulators may use fear to maintain the group's desired obedience and loyalty. To do this, the manipulator can threaten the individual's limb, life, or soul for anything against the new identity.

Deprivation of Sleep

If you don't have the sleep you need, you will often be vulnerable and disorientated. This can help to create the ideal environment the manipulator seeks during the brainwashing process breakdown and domination. Moreover, the victims are often required to do prolonged physical and mental activities in addition to insufficient sleep to speed up the process even more.

Dress Codes

Enforcing a dress code further removes the individuality of the victims and the choice they have to pick their clothing. Often, the victim is asked to wear the dress code held by the rest of the group during the brainwashing process.

Chanting

The agent works towards the elimination of any uncultured ideas in the mind of the victim. One way to do this is by chanting or repeating phrases used by those who follow the new identity.

Confession

Confession in people who are transforming from their old identity to the new identity is strongly encouraged. During this process, the ego's subject is destroyed by acknowledging to the agent the innermost doubts and personal weaknesses. Once you can let go of these things, the new identity can be introduced.

Pointing Your Finger

You will feel justified if you can point the finger at someone else. By merely pointing out certain flaws in the world, you are letting the world know that you are good. Before contrasting it with the benefits of the new identity to which the victim is directed, the manipulator may list all of the murder, prejudice, and gaps in the world.

5. Covert Manipulation

Covert manipulation is perhaps one of the more dangerous methods used in dark psychology. It involves systematically removing one person's power in such a secretive, deniable fashion that the individual typically never realizes it has happened. They may abruptly realize that they do not know how they have gotten to a specific point in their life, and feel so lost and confused, but unsure what to do. This is typically considered rather unethical, but it is important to understand.

Defining Covert Manipulation

When you attempt covert manipulation, you are attempting to learn what makes them tick so you can essentially dismantle them as a person and rebuild them into something completely different. It usually involves toying with insecurities so covertly, so secretly, that the other person never detects anything is happening. These acts are done in ways that allow for the manipulator to remain in control of the situation, but in a way that their relation to the event is deniable. This is done slowly at first, building up over time until the job is done.

To understand covert manipulation, you must understand what the words themselves mean. Covert refers to the secretive nature of the act—it is done entirely behind the scenes. The manipulator wants to remain the invisible puppeteer, pulling all of the strings while remaining as innocent as possible in the situation. This is done through hiding behind plausible deniability, meaning they can say that they did not do it and have it seemed reasonable and plausible that they did not. Secondly, you must understand what manipulation means— the act of swaying someone to do something that is not in their best interest and is not in line with their own free will.

Essentially, when you choose to covertly manipulate someone, you are hijacking their mind; you are secretly destroying everything they thought, they knew, and thought, while doing so behind their back in a way that leaves you innocent. You are turning them into little more than a puppet with no free will, convincing them to go along with whatever you may be desiring. You are essentially brainwashing someone else into obeying your commands, into doing what you see as beneficial for yourself and no one else.

It is necessary to note that you are essentially using them when you are attempting to covertly manipulate someone else into obedience. You are taking away their free will, their personality, and leaving behind a person that will obey. This is not something that you do to someone you love or value; it essentially dehumanizes someone.

Steps for Covert Manipulation

While quite insidious, the concept of covert manipulation is also quite simple: It involves 3 steps. If you are attempting to manipulate someone, you need to follow these 3 steps to ensure that it will be effective and to your benefit.

With the steps followed, you will be left with such an insecure and worried person about their capacity to think and make decisions that they will gladly defer to you out of ease. It is easier to follow along with whatever you are requesting than it is to make decisions on their own, and the person will do so. What is left at the end is the puppet that the manipulator has been trying to create. At this point, the manipulator can work on fine-tuning the target's actions, ensuring that bad behavior or not following through with what is requested is punished.

These 3 steps are the following:

1. Infiltrating the Target's Circle

The first step to covert manipulation is learning. You must learn all about the target to begin developing a weapons arsenal that will allow you to ultimately take full control over the other person. Start by attempting to be welcomed into the person's inner circle. You must be able to be befriended by the target if you hope to be close enough to manipulate.

This can be done by playacting to be interested—in a way you are. You are interested in learning what you can use later rather than interested in learning what makes the person tick simply to learn about the other person. When you are learning what they are interested in, and what makes them function as a person, you are feigning a bond between yourself and the other person. You want the other person to like, or maybe even love you, while you remain in control of the situation at hand.

Once you can develop the trust necessary to be welcomed into the inner circle of your target, you will start getting all the details you want and need. This is when you will begin learning more about the other person, and the more personal the details, the more likely you can use the details as weapons in the future.

2. Gather Your Weapons

As your relationship with the person, or rather the other person's attachment and trust to you, has grown, you will start to get the crucial details. You will likely learn all about the other person's family life, as well as sensitivities, beliefs, and other deep, personal thoughts that could be useful later.

At this point, you are learning all about the individual's weaknesses. You want to know where all of the chips in their metaphorical armor are, and exactly understand what you will need to do to turn that chip into a crack, and what you will need to do to make that crack shatter the armor as a whole.

In this, you are going to want to interact further with the target. You want to learn how to read their particular body language and tell as effortlessly as possible and what makes the person tick and work. This is when you begin to understand the other person's fears, thoughts, hopes, desire for the future, and anything else that may be offered to you. At this point, especially if you have been feigning interest in the relationship, or possibly even love bombing to push it forward, the other person will feel quite confident in the relationship. This is what you want—you want that comfort, that attachment, to build up, because that attachment is what will be your tether to keeping the person around, even through abuse and manipulation. When the other person is deeply attached, he or she will have a harder time separating from the abuse, even if it is discovered.

3. Break Down the Target

The last step to covert manipulation involves breaking down the target. At this point, you know the person as intimately as you may need to. You know what makes their minds work, their fears, strengths, and generally who they are. Then you are ready to begin chipping away at their self-esteem. Think of their self-esteem as their armor—the stronger it is, the less likely you will be able to install your strings to manipulate them. If you want an easy target for manipulation, you must destroy their self-esteem. At that time, he/she is not as likely to resist the manipulation or stand up to any abusive behaviors. They will get to trust your judgment; instead, losing the confidence in their behaviors that would have allowed them to stand up to you in an effective manner.

Remember, this process is gradual. If you start too big too quickly, the target will catch on and leave. Think of this as acclimating to water. If you are wanting to take a hot shower, you start with the water at a tolerable temperature and slowly work your way up to temperatures that would have been painful had you gone straight into them, and you would have jumped away from them. Your target will jump away from you if you attempt to go too big too quickly.

You could start with subtle jokes—things that you can innocently deny. For example, if you seek to manipulate your girlfriend into losing weight, you could comment about pregnant women shortly after poking her stomach. She might feel a little unconfident at the comment, and if she says something to you about it, you can shrug it off, say she must have been imagining the connection between the comment and the touch, and that she should not be so sensitive, or if she is that sensitive, maybe she should do something about it instead of sitting around and complaining.

This could then move on a step further—the next time your girlfriend goes for a dish that is unhealthy or wants a snack that is fatty or sugary, you could quirk a brow, almost in patronizing disgust and questioning her decisions without saying a word. She may then call you out on that as well, which again, you should deny, claiming you never looked at her like that. Remind her that you are not in control of her body or what she is consuming while speaking in a slightly disapproving voice. Considering she is likely to be insecure about herself at this point, you can slowly chip at her self-esteem without having to do anything extra. Even if you do not care about her weight, this is one of the easiest ways to chip at someone—people are typically the most insecure about their appearances, even if their appearances are perfectly fine in the first place.

Even further, the next time she orders something unhealthy at a restaurant, you could be slightly more overt, such as sighing in disapproval. When questioned, you continue to deny the action as being connected, instead of blaming it on a long day at work or something else innocuous. You want her to feel insecure enough about herself to instantly jump to conclusions, and also insecure enough to untrust her gut reaction when you are doing something that is intentionally meant to make her feel that way.

The last step toward degrading her further and shattering her self-esteem would be through actually saying something. You could make a comment about how she always complains about her weight, but she never does anything to fix it, and that clearly, she does not care about the extra weight she carries if she never made an effort to work it off. This last step is likely to be far more damaging than the rest, but the entire point here is to degrade her self-esteem slowly down to nothing. Once it is at nothing, you can begin to put her back together again, installing all of the strings and buttons you need her to have to control and manipulate her yourself fully.

Because this has been happening gradually for so long and you have repeatedly denied any involvement with the negative comments or dirty looks, your girlfriend is not likely to associate you with the personality changes that may be noticed. She may decide that she should be losing weight. She is also likely to be far more responsive when you do show subtle signs of displeasure. Even the slightest smirk or scowl, even if only for a split second, will be enough to instantly trigger that insecurity in your girlfriend, allowing for you to superimpose your desires and beliefs in place of her gut reaction.

6. What Is NLP, and How Is It Unlike From Manipulation?

What is NLP?

NLP, short for Neuro-Linguistic Programming is a set of techniques and beliefs that incorporate brain science, behavioral science, and patterns in order to help people achieve their goals faster. Some of the goals include changing behavior patterns to improve relationships, improving memory or reducing anxiety. There are different reasons for why someone may implement NLP techniques into their life. Some may be interested in the science behind it such as how it works and whether or not it can be used to make predictions. Others may want to learn specific behavioral techniques and beliefs. The most common reason why people learn NLP is to have a clearer mind, more effective communication, and more effective problem-solving skills. NLP has become a popular topic due to its simplicity of use and relatively low cost compared to other types of therapies that are commonly practiced in the mental health industry.

How NLP Works?

The NLP methods that are used in the therapy industry are often referred to as "techniques" or "techniques of change." It is relatively easy for a therapist to

153

state what results they have noticed from an individual and how others have responded. Other types of therapy may require a particular methodology like behavioral therapy or cognitive behavior that must be used in order for the patient to benefit.

The goal of NLP is not necessarily to get a person better, rather it wants them to be better at whatever they want to accomplish. The Golden Rule is one of many principles that can be incorporated into an NLP technique depending on the goals of the therapist or client. The goal of an NLP technique is to find a particular set of beliefs that will help the person achieve their goals in the best way possible. NLP is not unique in this sense, because most types of therapies try to find a particular set of beliefs. However, NLP does not necessarily use any other techniques besides finding these beliefs to change behavior patterns or help someone achieve their goals.

What Differentiates NLP from Other Types of Therapy on The Market Right Now?

The focus on belief systems above all else has resulted in a wide array of interest from people worldwide. NLP has been known to work with many different types of people and problems, but it is not necessarily a magic pill. When a person comes in to see an NLP therapist or attend a workshop, they will often tell you how many different techniques they have tried before – often times from several different types of therapy.

There are several ways that NLP can differ from other types of therapy on the market right now. Some of these techniques include the focus on language and grammar, the structure of an NLP session or therapy session, using eye movements for concentration exercises and belief systems as opposed to strictly behavioral therapies.

NLP is based on Neuro Science and therefore makes use of cognitive behavioral strategies in order to help clients achieve their goals. Those goals could be anything from career change to personal relationships. The goal of an NLP session or therapy session is to implement new language patterns that will help the client achieve their goals. This can be done in a number of ways such as using mirroring, hypnosis, identifying automatic thoughts, and reprogramming behavior patterns that are causing the client's issues.

There are many different beliefs that are used by NLP practitioners. Some of them include NLP as a science, evidence-based beliefs of NLP, rational beliefs of NLP, and other types of general or rational beliefs that are common in many different types of healing techniques including hypnosis, meditation and others more specific to behavioral therapy (e.g., cognitive behavioral therapy).

One of the most important beliefs used by NLP is the "Neuro-Linguistic Programming" (NLP) principle. The NLP principle states that a person's present circumstances have a direct correlation to their past experiences. This belief can be applied as a way to change the future rather than live in the past, and as a way to change past experiences into desirable current circumstances. This is often referred to as "future-focusing" because it encourages you to focus on goals in your life that are possible for your present self rather than dwelling in the past with undesirable events.

The NLP principle is also something that is often referred to as an "imperative belief" or even as a "prerequisite belief." It is one of the beliefs that is commonly and primarily used during NLP sessions. This allows for the practitioner to be more open to the process of practicing NLP. It may not always be possible to implement certain techniques in order for a session or therapy session to be successful, such as if a client has not yet had time in their life where they could have acquired certain techniques like mirroring. The NLP principle has often been used by therapists and clients alike to give them permission to practice any tools or techniques they may want implemented into their sessions or therapy sessions. This is because most people know that they will not be able to use NLP-type techniques until they are ready and fully prepared to make those changes on the inside.

A prerequisites belief can be associated with other beliefs such as "I have chosen this," or "this is all natural." It is important for clients to choose what they would like to use in their sessions and then accept their responsibility in building those new behaviors and attitudes.

This can be applied in a number of different ways when it comes to finding solutions for issues that people may have. It may be a belief that is needed to make a behavior change, or to allow for certain tools to be used with clients.

Some of the NLP beliefs have been used in psychotherapy for quite some time. However, NLP has added its own techniques and additional steps in order to provide a more comprehensive service for people with specific needs. This can also be referred to as "matching the client's needs" because almost any client can have specific needs that must be taken into consideration when treating them using NLP techniques. While these beliefs are not specifically created by the originators of NLP, they are what have been used and passed down from each era since its inception in the 1970s.

How Is NLP Different from Brainwashing?

The term brainwashing is defined as the forceful indoctrination of an individual in order for them to believe a certain ideology. For example, the public in China would be brainwashed into thinking that Mao Zedong was a great leader. In order for this to happen, the public would have to be convinced that Mao Zedong was a good leader. Once the Chinese citizens were indoctrinated into believing in Mao Zedong, they would follow his orders and go through great turmoil to do so. However, NLP is a subtle process of changing behavior patterns which does not involve force or indoctrination but rather through changing beliefs and attitudes in order for them to assist in desired behavior change.

What's The Difference Between NLP and Manipulation?

The main difference between NLP practices and manipulating people is that with manipulation manipulators use fear tactics to get what they want from you such as money or power. An example would be a sociopath who is threatening harm towards you, in order to get what he wants. NLP tends to use techniques such as linking and mirroring rather than fear tactics. While NLP is not totally free of manipulation it does have methods that help people keep their integrity while they do receive feedback and learn from their mistakes.

Another difference between NLP and manipulation techniques would be that with manipulation there is no way to understand why someone wants something from you. With NLP you can learn how the brain works, why someone acts the way they do, and what motivates them so you can interact better with them. Manipulators may use these tactics on a one-time basis, which can make it hard to understand what they really want from you. Manipulation tends to be used to control someone and get them to do something against their will. NLP is used more frequently, although it is not used on the same person. People who learn

NLP have the ability to use them on themselves, as well as others which makes it an extremely versatile form of training.

The Importance of NLP

Neuro-Linguistic Programming is not only necessary for the understanding of a person's being, but it also helps in the understanding of the way an individual is. It helps a person to get deep into the root cause of the problem, as well as the foundation of their being.

Here are some other reasons why NLP is important:

- It helps people take responsibility for the things that they feel they may not be able to control. With the help of NLP, a person can change the way they react to events of the past and have a certain level of control over their future.

- People need to be aware of the body language of the members of their inner circle, as well as those with who they seek to do business. With NLP, it is possible to make use of the language with both control and purpose, and with this, it is possible to have control over your life.

- Remember, you cannot expect to make the same mistakes using the same mindset and hope to get different results. During an NLP session, the focus is placed entirely on the client as they are made the subject. This helps a lot because, at the point where a person can deal with themselves, they gain more clarity into their dealings with other people.

- It helps to improve finances, sales performance, marriage, health issues, parenting, customer service, and every other aspect and phase of life. This is because it helps in the holistic improvement of an individual and when a person is whole, his interactions and relationship with himself and other people become whole as well.

- It assists in targeting your beliefs, thoughts, and values and helps with the targeting of a person's brain functions, as well as developing certain behaviors. It also shapes the way these behaviors metamorphoses into habits, and how the habits change to actions which in turn comes as results.

- NLP applies to different vocations and professions. This is a tool that is very important in the mastery of sales, personal development experts and self-help, teaching, communication, parenting, and other facets of life.

7. Stages of Hypnosis

Hypnosis is pretty easy to understand if you know how it works. Of course, it takes practice to master hypnotizing others; however, simply understanding how it works is very useful in being able to observe dark psychology and manipulation in practice.

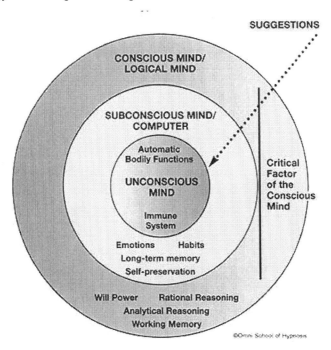

Hypnosis tends to be misunderstood as a parlor trick that requires someone to be asleep or in a nearly asleep state to become hypnotized. Then, when they are under the spell of hypnosis, they can be made to cluck like a chicken or bark like a dog, or repeat any number of embarrassing phrases for a cheap laugh. Hypnosis happens every day because all hypnosis means is that someone has entered into an altered state or a trance state.

Stage 1: Absorb Attention

The first step into altering someone's conscious state (hypnosis) is grabbing hold of their full attention. Believe it or not, there are verbal and non-verbal forms of this first stage of hypnosis. Take, for example, the situation mentioned above in which a person can be so zoned in at work that everything around them sort of just fades away.

This is a prime example of the way that our psychological states are changed when we are intently focused on something and of non-verbal hypnosis.

Of course, gaining someone's complete attention can be a bit easier if you are using words. People tend to cling more completely to someone's words when they are describing images or telling a story. It is a lot like how some people prefer visual learning over textual learning. The human mind can follow along better when pictures and mental images are involved because their visual sense is engaged.

You can practice this first stage of attention absorption in everyday speech. Go out with a friend or coworker and see how much more they pay attention to you when you say you have a story for them. Tell them a story, either true or made up, and be sure to include a lot of details. Paint the picture with your words, use a lot of adjectives to describe the scene. The more senses you can encompass, the better. Give their mind and imagination something to engage with.

When you have them wrapped up in your story, you have successfully absorbed their attention which will lead you into the 2nd stage of hypnosis:

Stage 2: Bypass the Critical Faculty

The conscious mind is a somewhat constrained being. It absorbs the information that is presented to you every day and rationally processes it. Contrarily, the unconscious mind is much more irrational. It does not become mired in real-world issues. Think about the fact that when you dream, your unconscious mind is engaged. Even if you've never really seen a purple, flying turtle, your subconscious mind is free to believe that such things are entirely real and possible. The conscious mind deals with what is feasible. In hypnosis, this is what is known as the critical faculty. Think of the critical faculty as a guardian at the gate to the subconscious mind. The critical faculty is what alerts your mind to things that are impossible, unreasonable, and unlikely. If you are attempting to hypnotize someone, the critical faculty is the enemy of hypnosis. The point of hypnosis is transferring a person's mind from a fully conscious state to an unconscious or at least an altered state, and the critical faculties make it impossible for this switch to occur, so it must be bypassed.

By capturing a person's entire attention first, it is possible to bypass their critical faculties. This can be done by adopting easy strategies like maintaining eye contact and speaking more slowly and subtly than usual. Bypassing the critical faculty and inducing a trance state can be accomplished in large part by speaking in a hypnotic manner. Watch out for indications that your subject is in a trance state if you're hypnotizing them. Most importantly, wait until you are positive you have passed the critical faculty and your subject is in a trance state before making any hypnotic suggestions. Otherwise, the critical faculty will reject your suggestion.

Step 3: Activate an Unconscious Response

It's not necessary to make someone cluck like a chicken to trigger an unconscious response. It can be as subtly effective as causing someone to giggle or put their palms to their mouths in surprise. An action that is done without the awareness of the person or of which the person becomes aware afterwards is referred to as an unconscious response. It is a response that has not been controlled by the conscious mind, to put it another way. When someone is in a hypnotic state, activating an unconscious response is quite simple. Look for changes in breathing pattern, dilated pupils, or skin flushing. All of these indicate that your subject has become hypnotized and has relaxed their guard about their critical faculties.

Once you notice this, try evoking an unconscious reaction. For example, you could describe in vivid detail a mouthwatering steak supper to make someone's stomach growl with hunger or a swarm of bugs engulfing someone's body to make their skin crawl.

Stage 4: Lead to Your Desired Outcome

This is the point where you, the hypnotist, can lead the subject towards the desired outcome through hypnotic suggestions or associated metaphors. This stage of hypnotism is all about speaking directly to the unconscious mind and taking advantage of the altered state to either help the person or to lead them to a conclusion, outcome, or decision that is favorable for you.

One example of this stage is called priming. Say, for example, that you want to go swimming and you want the subject to go swimming with you. Try telling them a story involving cool, cascading, and refreshing water overcoming oppressive heat. This could lead to a post-hypnotic reaction that has been geared towards your desired outcome.

Pattern Interrupts & Rapid Induction Techniques

The concept of pattern interrupts very simply. Consider each word individually: the first word in the phrase being "pattern." A pattern can be anything you do mindlessly or habitually. Getting up in the morning, brushing your teeth, and taking a shower is likely something you do every day that you don't even really think about. This is an example of a pattern. A pattern can also be called a routine. Getting in your car then driving to work can be considered a routine.

Now consider the second word in the phrase: "interrupt." An interrupt in this context is anything that breaks your normal routines or patterns. Interrupts are conscious efforts to change the way you do things, the way you think, or the way you act.

The major difference between the 2 words—the 2 concepts of "pattern" and "interrupt"—is that one involves an unconscious or passive state of mind, and the other involves a very conscious and active state of mind.

Pattern interrupts are often used in behavioral psychology and NLP to help people break harmful habits and routines in their lives. Routines often give us a sense of drive and purpose. Still, they can be detrimental when we get so used to them that we switch off our brains while doing them, thereby becoming vulnerable to hypnotic suggestion and manipulation.

The average human has about 50,000 thoughts per day, but the majority of these are repeat thoughts. Pattern interrupts are very effective ways to induce new thoughts, which helps the brain develop its ability to think critically. It is the difference between letting your brain atrophy and exercising it.

To get back to basics, consider pattern interrupts a way to alter your or someone else's mental state from a conscious to an unconscious mode. This is precisely why patterns can be used for hypnosis and NLP.

In particular, the pattern can be very useful for rapid hypnotic induction or getting someone into a hypnotic state very quickly. This may be because of a slight disconnect in a person's mind when a pattern interrupt is used on them.

The switch from passive to active brain function isn't seamless. There is a lapse in which the unconscious and conscious mind meld for a brief time, and it is in this time that a person enters a hypnotic state and is susceptible to suggestion.

Consider it a state of confusion that a person enters for a brief time when one of their patterns or thought processes is abruptly interrupted. Confusion tactics are very common and potent methods of rapid hypnotic induction.

Pattern interrupts and confusion are akin to polarization in the sense that both are used to get someone into a frame of mind where their reactions can be predicted and manipulated.

Getting someone riled up about a certain subject is similar to putting someone into a confused state where their routine has been suddenly broken. It is in this state that a skilled hypnotist can implant unconscious suggestions and therefore predict a certain outcome.

Pattern interrupt techniques have become very popular in hypnosis and manipulation because they are fairly simple to carry out, and they can be done in virtually any setting and sometimes without the person even realizing it. It happens in an instant and garners the desired results in an instant, which is why it has become such an oft-used tool to hypnotize and manipulate people.

The most popular method of pattern that interrupts hypnotic induction is the handshake technique. In this technique, the hypnotist will go in for the very mundane act of shaking someone's hand. At the last second, before the hand's touch, one person abruptly disengages from the handshake and grabs the other person by the wrist.

Getting up and getting ready for work is a routine that could take hours, and shaking someone's hand only takes a few seconds, but they are both patterns and they can both be broken, and when they are, the mind enters an altered state.

This altered state is the goal of pattern interrupts and why they are such a powerful tool for inducing hypnotic trances.

Using Pattern Interrupt to Induce Hypnosis

Pattern interrupts are just another means of grabbing someone's full attention, and it can be argued that hypnosis is nothing but getting someone to be fully present in the moment.

It can be as easy as interrupting someone mid-sentence. Let's say you get your friend telling you a story about a run-in they had at a grocery store or a confrontation they had with someone that bumped into them on the street. Try interrupting them in the middle of the story with an unrelated phrase, "I have always wondered what makes the moon so silvery."

There is an extremely simple way to manipulate people that pretty much anyone can do, but even this base tactic is an example of successful psychological manipulation through pattern interruption. Picture if you will, a situation in which your spouse is deep in thought about what to make for dinner. You want chicken, but you have no idea what your spouse is imagining making. Suddenly showing her a coupon in the paper or a particularly enticing video online for the chicken recipe can break their concentration on whatever type of food they were thinking of cooking and gets a new train of thought going on chicken. You have successfully used a pattern interrupt to manipulate the situation and heightened your chances of having chicken for dinner.

8. Mind Control Techniques to Be Aware of

Mind Control

For brain diseases, the ability to regulate electrical activation in brain pathways can do as an electrical activity has done to treat heart disorders. Researchers and physicians will cure various neurological and psychological conditions, from Parkinson's disease to persistent illness, by grinning electrical or magnetic stimuli across the scalp and by inserting electrodes in the brain.

Yet the idea of "mind control" horrifies many. There is a sordid history of brain stimulation to alter actions and cure mental illness. In the 1970s, Tulane University neuropsychologist name Robert Heath implanted stimuli into the brain of a gay man to "cure" him of his sexuality by activating his brain's pleasure core. In primates, individuals, and even a charging bull, a Spanish neuroscientist known as José Delgado utilized brain stimulation to explain how complex actions and functions are regulated at the level of a neural network and to control them at will by hitting the button on his radio-controlled system to energize electrodes embedded in the brain. Anything at Delgado's hands was manipulating actions, changing emotions, evoking images, anger, and zeal. Delgado's purpose was to rid the environment of deviant behavior by calming the brain and creating a "psych civilized" culture.

For many, the idea of electrical stimuli manipulating a person's brain is alarming. Still, existing techniques of treating psychiatric and neurological conditions are woefully ineffective and much too direct. Besides the one intended, neuronal and psychoactive medications manipulate several different neuronal pathways, triggering wide-ranging adverse effects. It can affect the brain and any cell in the body that reacts with the medications, such as SSRIs (Selective Serotonin Reuptake Inhibitors) for chronic depression treatment.

Medicines used to treat mental illness and medical problems are currently not often successful and are mostly administered in a trial-and-error manner. Psychosurgery also has a horrific history of violence, famously prefrontal lobotomy. Also, although any surgeon faces the danger of losing the person on the hospital floor, neurosurgeons face the unusual risk of saving the life of a patient but of losing the person. Surgical brain tissue extraction can damage healthy tissue or fail to remove all defective tissue in patients with physical, personality, cognitive, or mood dysfunction. Electroconvulsive stimulation (ECT) shakes the whole brain with seizure to cure severe stress and other psychiatric illnesses; the brain eventually adjusts itself in the aftermath of the electric firestorm, and sometimes people are aided, but not always, and sometimes there are harmful adverse effects, or the procedure fails to function.

It makes much more sense to activate the exact neuronal network that is malfunctioning rather than flooding the entire brain with bursts of energy or inundating it with narcotics. Doctors are also using the same approach to treat a wide variety of neurological and mental disorders, from scleroderma to OCD (Obsessive Compulsive Disorder), after brain stimulation's effectiveness in managing Parkinson's disorder. But they also do so at a neuronal circuit level without the necessary clinical explanation of the condition. For mental disorders, which are under portrayed among animals used in testing, this is particularly so. It's not entirely known how electrotherapy functions to improve these disorders, including Parkinson's disease. There is not always the requisite awareness of where to position the electrodes or what electrical stimulation intensity and pattern to use. In effect, these doctors do tests on their patients. They do it because it helps.

Without inserting electrodes inside the brain to cure mental illness and neurological disorders and enhance mood and cognition, non-invasive ways of altering brainwaves and electrical activity patterns in individual brain circuits, like neurofeedback, flashing light or rhythmic sound, magnetic and ultrasonic stimulation via the scalp, may alter neuronal activity. In the year 2008, the FDA (U.S. Food and Drug Administration) granted the treatment of depression by deep brain stimulation and subsequently extended clearance for pain and migraine treatment. An electrical current may be exerted to activate or prevent neurons from functioning in specific brain regions using an electrode on the skin. This methodology is used by the military to speed up learning and boost pilot's cognitive performance. The procedure is so fundamental that brain stimulation systems can be bought on the web, and you can create one from 9V batteries yourself. But the DIY ("Do it yourself") technique makes an innovative guinea pig to the consumer. New precision brain imaging methods are created. Electrical stimulation, taking the route of low resistance across brain tissue and activating nerves from remote brain areas that stretch axons past the electrode, is notoriously inaccurate. Quite specific induction or suppression of neuronal firing may be accomplished in laboratory animals by optogenetics. This approach uses genetic engineering to implant heat emitting signaling molecules into individual neurons to very effectively monitor their firing using laser light beamed through a fiberoptic cable through the brain. Applied to people, optogenetic stimulation through precise regulation of complex neuronal pathways could cure specific neurological and psychological problems but using this technique in humans is not morally justified.

Mind Control Techniques to Be Aware of

We have all encountered mind control as people in society and have used mind control techniques in one type or another. Whether it is under the pretense of persuasion, hypnosis, manipulation, or deception, we have all experienced or used it. To get us to support and vote for them, politicians use them. In general, our family, friends, or substantial others do use mind control methods to manipulate and persuade us whatever they want. For sure, if you concede to it or not, in an attempt to achieve an inevitable result, probably, you've also used mind control techniques. Mind control is not bad or good inherently, but it's how you use it, the motives behind it, and the outcomes it produces. If you use your mind with malicious intent, this can be considered evil.

Furthermore, it may also be regarded as bad if the result it creates is adversely harmful. However, it has been used for useful intentions if you employ mind management with goodwill. It generates beneficial effects for those concerned. Techniques of mind control are one thing and can be whether seductive or harmful depending on their use. To different people, they mean different things. They are also known, among others, as coercive persuasion, seduction, reform of perception, and manipulation. These all identities have common characteristics, primarily those that define the control of the mind.

However, each one relates to persuasion and direct or indirect effect on an individual's thoughts to walk into a particular role.

In interpersonal relationships, we addressed psychological coercion, described the distinction between manipulator and influencer, and listed potential risks or mental hot buttons that make you more prone to exploitation, and some signs and symptoms in an emotionally abusive relationship.

We will explore specific real methods of mind management that have historically been used by ordinary individuals in intimate interactions and communities.

Isolation

Physical isolation may be quite useful, yet manipulators may usually try to isolate you even though physical isolation is challenging or not realistic psychologically.

From one week of lectures across the world to criticize the family and group of friends, this can be done in various ways. The ultimate aim is to restrict all other power by regulating knowledge flow.

Critique

As an isolation technique, the critique can be used. In "us versus them" terminology, the manipulators will generally voice, condemn the exterior world, and assert their dominance. You must feel fortunate to be affiliated with them, as per them.

Social Proof and Peer Pressure

To brainwash immigrants, those who want to control large crowds may usually use psychological data and peer pressure. Social evidence is a cultural tendency where (some) individuals believe that other's behavior and attitudes are acceptable and that they must be validated because "every individual does that." This works very well when a person is unsure of what to say, how to feel, and what to do. Many people will just reflect on how others do and do the exact in those cases.

Fear of Being Alienated

Usually, outsiders to manipulative communities will obtain a positive response and develop various new partnerships that appear to be much more severe and significant than everything they have encountered. Later on, these partnerships will become a potent weapon to keep them in the community if any questions occur. And if they aren't entirely persuaded, life can seem very lonely in the outside world.

Repeating

Another effective persuasive tactic is relentless repetition. While it can sound too easy to be successful, it makes it recognizable and easier to recall by repeating the exact text over and over. When repetition is paired with social data, the message is conveyed without loss.

Significant evidence that repetition functions are the presence of assertions as a technique of self-improvement. If you can reassure yourself by consistency, the odds are that someone can try and use repetition to exploit you in some way to think and act.

Tiredness

Fatigue and lack of sleep result in mental and physical tiredness. You are much more prone to convincing when you're emotionally drained and less conscious. A Journal of Experimental Psychology research indicates that people who had not slept for just 21 hours were more open to suggestions.

Forming a New Identity

Inevitably, manipulators want the personality to be re-defined. They would like you to quit being yourself and become a robot who executes their orders mindlessly. Using all the tactics mentioned earlier and mind conditioning tactics, they will try to elicit from you a concession, some sort of acknowledgment that you think they are decent folk doing a positive thing (slight differences are possible). It could be something relatively trivial at the outset, such as accepting that the group members are fun and caring individuals or that their viewpoints are true. When you embrace the one tiny thing, you might be more likely to accept one again, then another one and another. Before you realize it, you continue to classify as one of the parties out of the need to be associated with what you say and do. If you realize that your statements have been documented or filmed, this is immensely powerful. In case you wondered, there is tangible verification of your new name.

Now you may be curious about "community" in your life after completing this. Are you being manipulated by them?

Let's imagine that you are part of Greenpeace. It all began with a little donation, then some sort of fun experience (many new mates), and before you realize it, you're sitting on a small boat protesting Shell's fracking in the polar area while putting your education and career on hold. What was going here? Has Greenpeace fooled you into doing this? Oh, no. They inspired you. Although they have got you to do things you would never imagine doing that before, Greenpeace does not use you for its benefit. They wanted you to do what they think is best (although viewpoints can differ), and you decided that there is no real advantage here.

The Usefulness of Strategies for Mind Control

Not all results of these methods of mind management are detrimental. In some cases, they are beneficial, as far as they are not intrusive or applied.

They can be highly helpful in many people's lives when diligent clinicians or counselors use these mind control strategies. They are excellent means of suppressing addictions, surviving stressful events, boosting self-esteem, and even toning down feelings of suicide or self-destruction.

In short, when the mind's management isn't all evil or included in self-serving reasons these strategies are just positive.

9. Mind Control in the Workplace

Successful entrepreneurs know that it isn't a question of pressurizing people to get results. Results happen as a consequence of someone wanting to achieve those results. Therefore, it makes sense that controlling the mindset of the worker is more important than controlling the speed at which they work. The speed factor will be brought about as a direct result of the mindset.

Thus, to get someone at work to respond in a very positive way, you have to examine what makes people positive. Some may embrace change within the workplace while others will back away from it and have almost a phobic response to it. That's because those with less confidence may be afraid of failure. You know that failure isn't an option, but they don't. You need to change the mindset very quickly when you find people are resisting doing what you have told them is needed to be done. Your approach is important. Just like entrepreneurs who first start with a vision, your vision projected onto others is vital because you need each one of your workers to be as keen to get the job done as you are.

The Power of Suggestion

What you might not be conscious of is that the suggestion is extremely strong. Suggest there is something wrong with the food in a restaurant and people will get sick—not because there's something wrong with the food but because they believe there is, and belief is very powerful indeed. If you want to control the mindset of workers, you need to have a vision and like other entrepreneurs, sow the seeds of that vision so that other workers share it.

Too many people think that the work ethic is that you have a hierarchy where the boss dictates everything and the workers just do what they are told to do. Times are changing very fast and people are getting more progressive in their thinking. The idea is that you have a boss, but that you want to work for him, and it takes great mind control to change having to do something to wanting to do something.

Take a work friend and try this. Think of something you know will make the workplace more efficient. Talk it over with him and be enthusiastic. Make the idea seem something that will make his life easier and see how quickly he jumps on the bandwagon and starts telling others about this idea. He may even have the decency to give you the credit for the idea, but good news spreads very fast if you have planted the seed into his mind.

Getting people to do things is much easier than you think. If you already know the mindset of the person, then it is even easier. Here are a few samples of the types of mindset you may come across in the office, together with mind control methods that will work.

- **Getting someone to do work below their status**: Sometimes people hate to do jobs that they feel are below the status of their job. The way to get around this is to get into their mindset in the right way. I found a great way of doing this. Start the conversation something like this. Congratulate the staff member for their achievements and make them feel that you are giving them real praise. As you turn to leave, say "Hey, Tracy, I was going to ask you, can you help me out with something…" Hesitate and then say, "It is okay, it doesn't matter."

- What you are doing is planting seeds. The member of staff knows that you value them, and you've just allowed them to do something nice for you. I would bet that 90% of the time, you can then ask them to do something below their status, as a favor and get a favorable response.

- **Needy with lack of self-esteem**: Make them feel great at all times because this gives them belief in you. Nobody wants to believe negative things about themselves, but if you have problems with self-esteem and someone feels you're worthy, you're going to remain worthy in your way, which means ultra-productivity. It also helps people that are needy to feel needed and helps to impact their self-esteem issues. I have seen many employees who had this kind of issue get through them, just by being boosted and pointed in the right direction.

- **Leader of the pack mentality**: Let them be a leader of the pack but control how they rally the troops. Give them a little leeway and increase it as and when they prove themselves capable. Make the goalposts clear because these are workers that will always want to reach just beyond the goal post. The problem is that they can annoy workers and cause waves, so let out the reins a little at a time, letting them know acceptable parameters and how to achieve the next level.

- **The sheep of the office**: These are the people who go to work every day, do as they are told, and don't make waves. The problem is that sheep will always follow the herd, so to control the minds of the sheep, you need a shepherd who makes them feel happy and knows about the rewards of loyalty and good service. The Chinese do this very well and you can learn a lot from their experience and use their work ethic to make sure there are no more sheep. You turn them into a workforce that wants to do more than just show up each day. They want to be productive and the person you choose as their leader will make their work-life so pleasant, they will even volunteer to stay on and work overtime for the sake of the cause.

Control the mindset and you control the mind and that's when you start to get things done. Huge magnates who have made their millions did so because they remembered that each cog in the wheel was every bit as important as the process. One worker who worked with Richard Branson said that the man brought a kind of energy into the workplace. You wanted to succeed because there wasn't any other way forward. His enthusiasm and his drive rubbed off on others to such an extent that they felt they were impelled to succeed. Now working for another company, he said that successful men were those who were always open to changes and that listened to others. He was right because until you do listen, you do not know the existing mindset of the workforce that you have and if you cannot draw the lines between the different types of people, you can never control the mindset of the masses. Richard Branson did and people who work for him are galvanized by the way he encourages them and also listens to their ideas, not thinking that his ideas are the only viable ones.

An Experiment in Mind Control

You have probably seen this in practice but not realized what a good example of mind control it is. Stand on a busy street and lookup. Continue to look and don't stop looking. Other people will join you and will also look up and then you will see a small crowd of people looking up, more and more will join you.

173

You have somehow tapped into the minds of the people around you and they are mimicking your action. You must have seen this at work. It is a very old trick. Now try something entirely different. Go into the office late in the morning and have a whole carrier bag full of peppers from the supermarket. Place it by your desk where people can see it. When they ask you why you have bought so much pepper, act surprised. "You didn't know about it?" Of course, they will answer that they didn't because there was nothing to hear about. "They are stopping the sale of pepper tomorrow because of a world shortage. I need mine for cooking. If you want any, you better act quickly because the shelves are getting empty."

By the time that you come back from lunch, you will find that many of the people in the office have secured their supply of peppers. Remember, something like pepper lasts for months, but chances are that they will have bought much more than any human being can consume within a year. If it didn't work where you are, think of something you know local people love to eat and try that. The entire point of this exercise is that you are controlling their thought processes and getting them to do something which is extremely off the wall just by suggesting it.

The suggestion is extremely powerful and when used correctly in the workplace it can give very good results. Think of ways in which suggestion can aid productivity because when you do, you will find that even the laziest of workers will respond because they see being productive as being enjoyable too. The way that you control the minds of the workforce is a great reflection of your leadership powers. An office that is mediocre and whose workers are dispirited maybe it is because they do not have the most dynamic of leaders. Instead of blaming the workers for their apathy, the mind controller will come up with ways to make the workplace more dynamic and boost the mindset of those around, so that they find great joy in doing more than they normally would. When the success of the workplace equates to personal satisfaction, workers will answer the way you wanted, and productivity will soar.

There are lots of ways that you can use these tips and tricks in relationships as well. Remember the sequence.

- Know your subject.
- Know how they think.

- Change your approach to fit how they think.

- Sow the seeds.

- Watch them respond in the way you anticipated.

- Voila! You get results.

You may think that it is completely coincidental that people react in a certain way to certain criteria, but it isn't. There are set behavioral patterns and if you have ever watched a magician at work, what he is doing is playing with the audience, bearing in mind the set way that people respond to certain stimuli. He could be doing something transparent to someone studying magic, but to the average person watching it will look as though the trick is magic. These are people who read other's minds in a very shrewd way and come up with a great result, and their magic looks real even to skeptics.

10. Techniques of Persuasion

Persuasion techniques can often go under other names and are also referred to as persuasion strategies.

The representative might talk to the subject while giving evidence to change the subject's mind, they could use some force or pull they have against the subject, and they can perform some services for the subject, or use other tactics.

Use of Force

Depending on the situation, the representative might choose to use some force to convince the subject to think like them. This may happen if the ideas do not match up correctly, regular talking is not working, or when the agent is becoming frustrated or upset with the turn of the conversation.

Force is often used as a type of scare tactics because it provides the subject time to think rationally about what is going on when a regular conversation takes place, compared to the force that will be used when the representative has had less success using the other means of persuasion that are given. However, starting with power, in some cases, is excellent. Sometimes, force may be used if the agent seems like they are losing control or when the subject can present inconsistent evidence to the agent, and the agent ends up being angry.

When it comes to the procedure of persuasion, it is not often the best idea to use force because many subjects will see the use of power as a hazard when they see that the representative will not offer other options to their demand.

The whole appeal of persuasion is that it left the subject with a choice. However, if force is involved the liberty of option is gone, and the subject is more likely to feel threatened. If they feel threatened, they are less likely to listen and think about anything the agent is saying; therefore, the process may not proceed because of these reasons.

The use of force is generally dissuaded, and it should be avoided in the process of persuasion, unlike the other forms of mind control.

Weapons of Control

Another technique that can be used to encourage the subject to lean a specific way is to use the weapons of control.

Weapons of control that can make the agent effective in their purpose are commitment, reciprocity and consistency, material evidence, scarcity, preference, and authority. These 6 weapons of influence are very crucial to the representative, considering that they are part of the process of change in their subjects. Let's see 2 of these weapons.

Reciprocity

The first weapon of control is the principle of reciprocity. This concept postulates that when a single person, the agent, gives the other person, the subject, something of value, the subject will try to pay back in kind. This generally applies when the agent performs some type of service, the subject will feel they have an obligation to render a comparable service to the agent for a long time. While the 2 functions might not equal, they have the same kind of worth so that the responsibility of each is equated out.

The act of reciprocation winds up, producing a sense of responsibility in the subject, which the representative will use as a powerful tool when they wish to use persuasion. The rule of reciprocity is very efficient because it assists the representative get the subject into the right mindset by instilling and subduing the subject with a sense of commitment. The representative may likely get the subject persuaded to do or act a particular way because the subject will have that sense of responsibility hanging over them.

Another advantage for the agent in using reciprocity is that it is not just a moral standing that will put the obligation on the subject; it is also a standing that is held up by social codes. The agent does not need to worry whether the subject will return the favor if they do not feel like doing so, the agent has some tools available to get this action.

As a community, people do not like individuals who are irresponsible in returning a favor or payment when they are given a gift or service. If the representative does not feel like the subject is going to pay back to them, they will be able to inform the social group. They can tell other buddies or colleagues how they favored the subject, but the subject did not return it when it was needed. Now the agent has forced social requirements on the subject, making it look like they will urge the subject to do something.

For the most part, the subject will be more than happy to reciprocate to the agent without requiring any outside forces. When the favor is given, the subject will begin to look for ways to pay back the agent not to seem greedy or self-centered. The representative will then have the ability to supply an option to the subject on how to repay this debt; the subject will feel appreciation for having this easy option and will likely go the way the representative desires.

Consistency and Commitment

The next weapon of control is commitment and consistency. The agents need to use both of these if they wish to convince anyone to change their point of view. They are much easier to understand and can assist the subject in making their choices much better when things are consistent. It refrains from doing well for the agent to change the facts that they are using continually or to change other info that is needed to help the subject process the details. Instead of assisting with the procedure of encouraging, always avoiding consistency is going to make the representative appear like a phony and someone who cannot be trusted, leading to the failure of the persuasion process.

Consistency is one of the most crucial aspects of the persuasion procedure. This is because:

- Consistency is highly valued in society: most times individuals like to have things remain a certain way. While there are many varieties in day-to-day life, individuals feel safe knowing that everything will stay pretty constant. It allows them to remember what has happened, know what to expect, and be prepared if any changes occur.

- If there were no consistency, things would be hard to plan, and there would always be confusion walking around. If you want to encourage a subject on a particular item, then you should ensure that your facts correspond and make sense to them.

- Consistency results in benefiting the everyday life of most individuals. Have you ever tried to prepare a day when something unexpected shows up?

- It can make things difficult and it may wind up feeling like a disaster.

Individuals like consistency because it allows them to understand what will happen and what to do. They know when it is time to eat, when it is time for work, and when other things will happen throughout the day.

- Consistency provides a shortcut that is very important for daily problems. Life is hard enough without needing to include other things that do not make sense. When people can have eternal experiences, it makes things easier.

- Consistency gives the subject the ability to make the right choices and to process details. They need to be sure their message is consistent if the representative wants to be successful to persuade the subject. There is no room for wrong proof that can appear later and mess up the entire procedure. Keep the facts concise and sincere, and it is far better for convincing the subject.

Something that connects consistency is the act of commitment. To understand that the subject is convinced, it is essential to have some type of commitment in place.

In marketing, this can mean that the subject is going to buy the product, or in politics that the subject will vote for this candidate. It varies depending on the nature of the persuasion.

According to the principle of consistency, if an individual makes up his mind to do something, either in writing or verbally, they are likely to honor the decision they made.

It has been found that this is more real in terms of written commitments given that the subject will be more concrete emotionally, and there is some strong evidence that they accepted the dedication. This makes a lot of sense; many individuals will guarantee that they will fix something or do something, just to reverse and refrain from doing it. Some people will do what they said, and they are more likely to do it if said than not promising at all; however, it is still tough to get the results that you desire in this way. Also, there is no chance to back it up given that an oral agreement will just end up being what they said, and no one would win. On the other hand, if the representative can produce a dedication from the subject, they have the proof they need that the important things have been done.

The factor that it is so important for the representative to get the subject to agree to a dedication is because, as the subject dedicated to the brand-new attitude, they have more propensity to act in such a way that is fitting to that commitment. After that point, the subject will advance and begin to participate in self-persuasion for the cause. They will supply themselves in addition to others with many reasons to support the commitment to avoid any issues with the agent. If the representative can work on that point, the representative will have a lot less work to handle.

Social Proof: Persuasion is a type of social interaction, and therefore it is going to follow the social rules where it is happening; the subject is going to be influenced by the people around them.

They will be willing to do what others are doing instead of doing their own thing.

The subject will base their beliefs and act according to what others are doing around them, how these same individuals act, and how they believe.

If the subject grows up in a city, they are likely to act like others who are from that city; on the other hand, those who grow up in a very spiritual neighborhood might spend most of their time praying, learning, and helping others.

Under this belief, the saying "the power of the crowd" can be true. The subject is going to know at all times at other individuals around them are doing. In this country, it has nearly become a fascination to do what others are doing, even though people will say how they want to be different and be an individual.

Do what others are doing can be shown with an example. If the host says, "Operators are waiting, please call now," the subject may feel like operators are sitting there because no one is calling them for anything. This will make the subject not call because they figure if another person is not calling, then they should not either. If the host just changes some words and instead says, "If operators are busy, please call again," there can be a different result. The subject is now going to assume that the operators are hectic with the calls of many other subjects, so the product needs to be excellent. The subject will likely call at once and not postpone it.

11. Psychological Persuasion Tips

Dark Psychology is a whole field of study that studies the methods and techniques of psychological persuasion. It is this field that we're going to be focusing on in this article, as it's a topic that affects us all every day.

Think about it: When was the last time you didn't see an advert on TV or online? When was the last time someone tried to sell you something in person? And when was the last time you saw a government campaign encouraging people to vote or donate money to charity? Chances are, these things have happened at some point in your life - and they were using one or more of the tactics we'll be discussing.

It is necessary to differentiate healthy social control from psychological exploitation. Good mutual influence exists between most individuals, which is part of the give-and-take of constructive partnerships. In psychological conditioning, one individual is used for the advantage of another. The manipulator intentionally establishes an inequality of influence, then uses the victim to fulfill her or his agenda.

Deception becomes a selfish act of coercion and, in the worst situations, abuse, sometimes beginning off as a competitive or survival instinct for self-preservation. Self-awareness, honesty, competence, proactive problem-solving capability, effective communication, and social skills are clear alternatives to deceptive capacity.

Why are you making the decisions you take or doing the stuff you do? There's always a cause, and psychologists are finding that in ways we don't know, much of our behaviors are affected and that these influences may be a very large variety of stuff. Also, modest persuasion may have a huge effect on us. You will realize that you need to encourage others to engage in you or work with you in the fulfillment of your dreams. Or you might like someone to see your side of things for one reason or another. Knowing how to use psychology to convince people may be a powerful asset in these cases, as in several other related ones.

But when you try to sway someone, it is necessary to be responsible and polite. Persuasion isn't the same as tampering. For positive motives, persuasion is performed to demonstrate others' views to eventually get them to cooperate with you or compromise with you. Manipulation is carried out with ill purpose, which typically includes deception or tricks to force others to consent or cooperate with it. It's deceit whether you're not saying the entire story or distorting the facts to persuade others to do something that would help you but maybe troublesome for them. It's persuasion to nudge people to see your side, so they are likely to comply with you. Persuasion is not forceful, it is not manipulative, and it is not damaging to people's persuasion. When applying the following suggestions in your life, bear this in mind.

Ultimate Terms

Some phrases are more convincing than others. To reassure you more easily, phrases defined as "ultimate concepts" may be inserted into your statement or pitch. They are divided into 3 categories: terms of God, terms of the devil, and charismatic terms. The words of God are also known as words of power and appear to be positive and appealing. For, e.g., if you are talking about safety, "guarantee" and "confirmed" are some similar God terms. The devil's words, on the other hand, are more pessimistic and repulsive to the public. A few that can be used are "dangerous" and "risky "for the same protection example. Then there are charismatic phrases that are a little trickier; because of historical meaning, concepts such as "democracy" or "development" are typically somewhat vague yet enticing. All the words in these definitions will also affect how people think about a topic or point of view and sound about it. They prompt particular responses because, through the course of our lives, we have been conditioned by practice to interpret certain terms in a certain manner. To build attraction and pull others in or to make an alternative solution seem impractical, you may use these types of terms.

Talk Rapidly

The presentation of the terms you've picked often influences the individual's responses to them. It helps in convincing for a couple of reasons as you talk fast. First, communicating rapidly suggests that to maintain pace with you, the person listening needs to comprehend what you're saying rapidly. It allows them patience to hear from you, but it makes it difficult for them to nitpick your point. They may always have major concerns, but they will be too busy reacting to and processing what they identify with it to disturb you to point out irrelevant information. Talking immediately will help you feel more assured, as well. Speaking softly and fumbling for the correct term will damage your pitch, but if you can talk smoothly at a very rapid speed, but not so rapidly that you are challenging to comprehend or follow, you are viewed as assured and competent, consciously or subconsciously by the people listening. When they perceive you as possessing certain characteristics, even if they don't know precisely why you cater to them, they are more prone to want to get to your team.

The Correct Body Language

Your body talks volumes alongside your thoughts. Like communicating fast, the people you're talking to actively consider your position and gestures, but they may only subconsciously take notice, which slightly may change their perception of you. Step up straight and calm, shoulders back. Do not fiddle with your thumbs, yet to emphasize your passion, use hand motions sometimes. Don't gaze down on the floor or at notes; maintain eye contact; instead, just don't keep that with a single person so steadily that it becomes disturbing. Looking positive shows people that you do what you do and know what you're talking about, non-verbally. It would leave an impact that makes individuals continue to help you and your endeavors and make them more willing to seriously consider you in an argument.

Repetition

Have you ever listened and not particularly enjoyed a song for the first time, only to come to appreciate it later after listening to it many more times? The human brain likes familiarity and trends because we can come to appreciate it more or embrace it more quickly when we're subjected to a concept often than when we first encountered it. So, reiterate the relevant detail 2–3 times while you're pitching a strategy or idea. For starters, if you want to persuade others of a product's quality, reiterate its efficacy stats in contrast with other comparable items. Present a concept in multiple forms in the conversation, whether you're in a friendly debate with a peer or colleague. They do not know they've just learned the same thing more than once, so they're more apt to start noticing the viewpoint, and their brain may take note. It's good to hold it 3 times in this kind of situation; if it's the same data replicated many times, rather than subtly converted with the same key concept, it will potentially trigger the reverse impact and make the user feel more resistant to it.

Balanced Arguments

There are very few ideal ideas; there may be a mistake or 2 in all the greatest proposals, principles, and thoughts. Although you might believe that the only approach to reassure someone is to concentrate solely on the positives and try to brush out all possible drawbacks, evidence has shown that people react better to balanced arguments. Many people would search for the flaws in it as a concept is pitched; if you do not recognize apparent defects, they may see you as dishonest. Or, if they don't see the drawbacks but believe the proposal is too amazing to be real, they're likely to have difficulty trusting you, and it's going to be tough to convince them. On the other hand, experiments have shown that two-sided claims are more effective in convincing, perhaps because you seem more trustworthy about your authenticity regarding the less favorable angles of your proposal. People are attracted to someone they know they can trust, and if you go that way, they are more inclined to listen to you.

Tell a Story Instead of Reporting Details

People respond to private encounters. A Carnegie Mellon University research contrasted the potency of 2 separate types of pitch. In both, students tried to collect donations to improve the quality of life of individuals experiencing food shortages, droughts, and dislocation from their homes in different African countries. To explain how poor the condition was, one pitch centered on facts and percentages, while the other pitch told the tale of a hungry girl called Rokia and included an image of her. More than twice as much money was collected for the cause by the students who used the tale. The result was that numbers are impersonal and would leave us feeling detached from the idea while people try to get involved by keeping it personal. You do not have to tell a tale of anyone else, actual or imagined; you can also clarify to someone on a specific level how your proposal impacts their existence. It's helpful to meet the person you are seeking to convince in a personal way.

Taking Away Some Strength From the Powerful

Being ready to take some of their influence away will help convince them to consider your side of things while offering a proposal to someone with greater power than you, like your manager, a powerful business owner, or a representative of some sort. Maybe this sounds a little grim, but it isn't. The entire premise is that often influential persons realize that they are powerful and appear to look down on individuals who are in a lower role. Although, by introducing them to unfamiliar items, you will steal some of their power; prove to them that in the topic you are talking about, you are more experienced than them by providing facts that they are unlikely to be acquainted with. They'll feel less effective if you're the most experienced in the case. Then, inform them of their position of influence and help them feel more comfortable about their appraisal of your pitch at the end of the discussion. For representatives of all sorts, that's a brilliant tactic, but it may be helpful in debates with individuals who feel dominant too.

When convincing is a desirable ability, there are several cases. Knowing tactics on a psychological basis that influence the audience can make you convince you more efficiently.

12. The Art of Deception and Mind Games

Deception

What is deception? It is the act of causing someone to believe something untrue. We all practice deception in one form or another. Some lies are bigger than others, telling your partner that you could never cheat on them is a big one for example. Telling your friend that she looks great in those jeans could just be a way of sparing her feelings.

Deception is not always practiced by other people. We can often self-deceive to preserve our self-esteem. Telling ourselves that we can achieve certain goals when all the evidence points to the fact that we can't is a healthy form of deception, but self-deception can lead to serious delusions.

While it is an accepted fact that we all use deception, it is a personal choice as to the nature of your lies. The trick is to be able to recognize deception in others.

This means that if we know the giveaway signs that tell us we are being lied to; we can avoid displaying them if we choose to practice deception.

What Are the Classic Signs That Someone Is Deceptive?

Lack of Self-Reference

When people are telling the truth, they use the pronoun "I" to describe their actions. For instance, "I left the office at 6:30 PM and I arrived home 20 minutes later. I then had a cup of tea and watched television."

This statement contains 3"I" pronouns and is probably true.

Deceptive people will avoid referring to themselves in this way and will use passive vocabulary when describing a situation.

Verb Tense

Truthful people describe events in the relevant tense. Historical events in the past tense indicate truthfulness, but a deceptive person will tell a story in the present tense.

For instance, when describing an encounter with a customer this employee indicates deception.

"She jumps out at me and grabs the dress. She is running out of the store and we try to follow her, but she is gone. She yells "loser" on the way out and is laughing all the time."

Avoidance

Even the most practiced liar will avoid voicing an outright lie for fear of detection. Dodging questions is a sure sign that somebody is trying to hide something. Replacing answers with questions is also a sign of deception.

"Do I look like the type of person who would do that?"

"Why would I tell you a lie?"

Vagueness

When we are speaking the truth, we are more definite with our speech. We state facts because we know they are true. Deceptive people use vaguer terms and fill their speech with vagaries. Using non-committal phrases such as "I guess,""sort of," and "I suppose," coupled with adverbs like "almost,""mainly,""around,""possibly," and "maybe" are a giveaway that their statement is untruthful. An unwillingness to be more direct can indicate deception.

Oaths

Do we believe that prefacing a statement with the phrase "I swear to God" makes us seem truthful? The opposite is true. Using oaths to back up your facts will only make you appear insincere and deceptive. When people are stating the truth, they rarely feel the need to sprinkle their speech with utterances like "As God is my witness" or "I cross my heart and hope to die."

Minimizing the Severity of Actions

When people are being questioned about incidents that have caused harm to others or distress, they can often use a term that makes the action seem less serious. Deceptive people who are accused of theft will often refer to borrowing or missing items. Threatening behavior can be described as a simple warning.

When telling the truth, we will use the term that fits the severity of the situation and not attempt to distort the facts.

Alluding to Actions

Being vague is a common indication of deception and when someone merely alludes to action it confirms a degree of untruth about their statement.

Speech is not the only way we can detect deception. Certain actions and changes in body language will tell us we are being lied to.

Head Movements

When someone is telling you an untruth, they will tend to change the position of their head. When asking somebody a question observe their head movements, if it is tilted back, bowed down or cocked chances are they are not being truthful.

Breathing

We all know how polygraph machines work by registering a change in heart rate and blood flow. What if you don't happen to have a polygraph handy? The breathing pattern of a liar will change because of the heart rate and blood, and they will begin to breathe heavily.

Mouth

A telltale sign that someone is lying is when their hand covers their mouth. They are using a primal form of cutting off the conversation and are showing their unwillingness to tell the truth.

Cover up!

Another giveaway sign of deception is when someone covers a vulnerable part of their body with their hand. The front of the throat is a key area to watch for. If the person you are talking to places their hand in that area chances are, they are lying.

Feet

Shuffling of feet is an indication that the speaker cannot wait to leave the situation. Honest people do not jiggle up and down and shuffle, because they are comfortable with the situation.

Blinking

When honest people speak, they blink normally. Deceptive individuals will try and convince you they are telling the truth by maintaining eye contact. Lack of blinking and a cold, steady gaze will tell you that you are being lied to.

Another way to spot lying is rapid blinking!

In psychology research, deception is a highly debated ethical issue. Some psychologists argue that deceiving people that participate in a research study is dishonest. Yet they cannot deny its effectiveness.

Kinds of Deception

Deception is a kind of interaction that depends on non-inclusion and also hinges on the order, to encourage that the topic of the globe fits ideally with the representative. Considering that there is interaction included, there will certainly additionally be several various sorts of deception that can be taking place. According to the Interpersonal Deception Theory, there are several sorts of deception that are discovered. Several of these have been displayed in the various other types of mind control, revealing that there can be some overlapping. Some primary types of deception are described next.

Exists

This is when the representative comprises details or offers details that are different from what is the fact. They will certainly provide these details to the topic as reality as well as the topic will certainly see it as the fact. This can be unsafe because the topic will certainly not recognize that they are being fed incorrect info; if the subject recognized that the details were incorrect, they would certainly not likely be speaking with the representative, and no deception would certainly take place.

Misrepresentations

This is when the representative will certainly make inconsistent, unclear, or indirect declarations. This is done to lead them based on obtaining overwhelmed as well as to not comprehend what is taking place. It can likewise assist the representative to preserve one's honor if the topic returns later on. It also makes them responsible for the incorrect details.

Camouflages

This is just one of the most typical sorts of deception that are utilized. Cover-ups are when the representative leaves out info that matters or essential to the context, deliberately, or they take part in any kind of actions that would certainly conceal details that relates to the topic for that specific context. The representative will certainly not have straight existed to the topic; however, they will certainly have seen to it that the essential details required never make it to the topic.

Disguise

When info is kept from the topic, it shadows how they can believe considering that they do not have the ideal details to make rational options. While the topic might believe that they are making sensible options of their very own free choice, the representative has eliminated essential info that might alter the topic's mind.

Simulation

Another element of deception is referredto as simulation. This includes revealing the subject info, which is incorrect. There are 3 strategies that can be used in simulation, consisting of perturbation, construction, and mimicry.

In mimicry or the duplication of an additional version, the representative will certainly be automatically portraying something that resembles themselves. They might have a suggestion that resembles another person's as well as opposed to providing credit history, they will certainly state that it is all their own. This kind of simulation can frequently happen via auditory, aesthetic, as well as various other methods.

Construction is an additional device that the representative might make use of when utilizing deception. What this indicates is that the representative will certainly take something that is located as well as transform it to make sure that it is various. They might narrate what did not occur or include decorations that make it seem far better or even worse than it was. While the core of the tale might hold true, yes, they did obtain a negative quality on an examination, it is most likely to have some additional points placed in such as the educator provided a negative quality purposefully. The truth is that the representative did not examine which is why they obtained the poor quality, to begin with.

Ultimately, diversion is one more kind of simulation in deception. This is when the representative attempts to obtain them based on concentrated fact, normally by baiting or providing something that may be a lot more alluring than the reality that is being hidden. As an example, if the hubby is ripping off and believes the spouse is beginning to discover it, he might earn a ruby ring to sidetrack her from the problem momentarily. The problem with this technique is that it usually does not last long as well as the representative has to discover an additional method to trick the topic to maintain the procedure going.

Overestimation

This is when the representative will certainly overemphasize a truth or extend the fact a little to transform the tale how they would certainly such as. While the representative might not be straight existing to the topic, they are most likely to make the circumstance appear like a larger offer than it truly is, or they might alter the fact a bit to make sure that the topic will certainly do what they desire.

Exaggerations

An exaggeration is the specific reverse of the overestimation device because the representative is most likely to minimize or lessen facets of the reality. They will certainly inform the topic that an occasion is not that huge of offer when, as a matter of fact, maybe the important things that establish whether the subject finishes or obtains that huge promo. The representative will certainly have the ability to return later on as well and state just how they did not recognize how huge of a bargain it was, leaving them to look great and also virtually a minor if they grumble.

PART III.

Defense and Healing

13. Traits of Emotional Intelligence

Emotional intelligence is not a topic that is typically talked about in normal settings like school or even at the kitchen table. Therefore, it is inevitable that more oven than not that a person suffers from emotional illiteracy compared to being emotionally intelligent. However, gaining emotional intelligence extends beyond reading and the classroom. It goes beyond acknowledging the importance of developing emotional intelligence.

It first comes with an acceptance that there is a need for change. Embrace that there is room for improvement in this area because no matter how far you have come in understanding and positively responding to emotions, there is always more that can be done. This is because your emotional brain is always changing. It changes structurally to accommodate the new things that you learn and to create memories of the lessons that life teaches you.

You have the power to guide that change in a positive manner that encourages emotional growth rather than hindering you no matter how you were raised or what relationships you were entangled with. Always remember that you have the power of choice. Remember that the ball when it comes to controlling and managing your emotions always remains in your court.

To ensure that you utilize that power to its full advantage, there are skills that you must develop to increase your emotional literacy. Just like verbal literacy begins with building blocks like learning the alphabet and basic grammar and vocabulary, emotional literacy begins with its own unique set of building blocks. By learning these basic skills, you can create a strong foundation that is the pillars of infinite possibilities and success.

Characteristics That Display High Emotional Intelligence

The basic traits you need to develop to be emotional intelligent are:

Self-Awareness

Being self-aware is the ability that a person develops to observe themselves—

thoughts, feelings, and actions—from a neutral, clear, and objective point of view. The point of becoming self-aware is to realize that you are separate from your emotions and thoughts and, thus, you are the one in control of your actions and behaviors. It is about elevating yourself so that you are not controlled by your thoughts and emotions.

Self-awareness is a spectrum ability, whereby you can attain different levels of it. Therefore, everyone has a certain amount of it. The ability to get on the more end of that spectrum where you are more aware than not of what happens in your mind and heart is what you should shoot for an emotionally intelligent person.

Introspection

To develop the ability of self-awareness, you first need to be able to look internally and reflect on what goes on in your internal environment. Human beings are complex creatures. That is the only way that you can have such diversity on a planet where there are billions of people. We are a mirage of thoughts, feelings, emotions, and experiences, all of which make us unique.

Thus, our minds carry the same characteristic. Our minds are a mix of good, bad, and ugly. Therefore, the ultimate goal should be to minimize the bad and ugly even though there is no getting away from their existence. To accomplish that, you need to learn to introspect so that identification of the things that need to change can be made.

Do not shy away from the things that make you. Even the bad and ugly stuff is part of what makes you such a unique and beautiful creation. Embrace them then tame them. Introspection gives you the power to do that.

Being Observant

In a time when everything is done in the fast lane, people tend to only observe things on a surface level. We have been taught to move just as quickly and so, we often do not take the time to stop and smell the roses. We have also been taught that we always need to be in the thick of things even when there are times when taking a step back and just looking is more beneficial.

Being observant requires a mindset shift and admitting that the details of the here and now are significant. Taking action is not always the best. Sometimes it is best to look before you leap and being observant allows you that benefit.

Self-Discipline

The ability to control your emotions despite the temptation to do otherwise is known as self-discipline. The progress you make in your life is the sum of the decisions that you make and being self-disciplined gives you the power to stick to the decisions that you have made and follow through with powerful action so that you can achieve your goals. The power of self-discipline is that it allows you to resist the urge for instant gratification and pleasure so that you can gain more satisfying rewards in the future based on the time and effort that you place into accomplishing your goals.

Again, we live in a society that is based on getting things here, now, and fast, and therefore, self-discipline seems to be something that is being left in the dust. However, self-discipline is a major requirement for learning to handle and manage your emotions.

Motivation

Being emotionally intelligent means that a person is dedicated to growing and developing themselves in their entirety (physically, mentally, emotionally, and spiritually) in addition to crashing through any obstacles that will inevitably get in the way of that development. Many people spend their days wasting away in a conundrum of thoughts and feelings that have no direction. Those thoughts and feelings manifest themselves in the way that the person acts and approaches life. One day, they are passionate about something, and the next day they are not. One week, they are highly motivated to pursue a particular course of action, and the next week they are not. One month, they are sure that these and that are the things that define them and dedicate all their focus and energy to pursuing these things, and the next month they are not.

Such people typically are not aware of their life purpose and therefore, have no drive to achieve any particular course. This is why they find themselves year after year stuck in the same position and unsure why that is. Being emotionally intelligent allows a person to recognize there is more to life than just existing or living to the next day. An emotionally intelligent person actively works on finding out their purpose in life and thus, makes efforts and puta in energy to attain that purpose. This person will only be able to do so if they are personally motivated.

Habits

Repeated patterns of behavior that shape our lives such as the time that we wake up and go to sleep, how we approach goal setting and planning, and even the propensity for nail-biting. These repeated behaviors are known as habits. Conducts can be good or bad and the brain tends to favor having them because it is less strenuous as fewer decisions are required to be made.

We have noticed that emotional illiteracy relies on several bad habits such as procrastination, however, you still have the power to turn this around and develop good habits that propel your life in a progressive direction. You can accomplish this progression with conscious and deliberate effort instead of relying on old behaviors that do not aid your growth and self-development.

Communication

It is not enough to know your emotions. As an emotionally intelligent person, you need to be able to articulate and express them to other people effectively and efficientlywhich gets your point across. Therefore, having good communication skills is important so that you develop an edge in emotional intelligence that takes you past just being familiar with your emotions.

Effective communication is not just about speaking, having good language skills, or getting your point across. You also need to be able to receive the message that other people are sending across to you as well. This is why so many people have to deal with drama daily in the different relationships that make up their life. Miscommunication often occurs in different settings of life because we do not know how to step out of ourselves or away from our emotions to effectively receive the message that other people are trying to get across to us.

Getting that message that means being able to be an active listener. Most people do not understand that there is a difference between hearing and listening. Simply hearing leaves, a person in a position to interpret the things that are being communicated to them as they will or desire, but actively listening allows a person to better comprehend what another person is trying to communicate to them. Being a good effective listener allows you to not allow your feelings and emotions to get in the way of the communication that is taking place so that you can approach communication with a more neutral and unbiased technique.

Empathy

Being emotionally smart is not just about being able to recognize and, therefore, effectively deal with your own emotions. It is also about being able to recognize and handle the emotions of people who are around you. While you should not shoulder the emotions of other people, being able to recognize their emotions helps reduce misunderstandings during communication. Therefore, it is imminent that you learn to recognize body language, facial expressions, and an instinct as to what other people might be feeling.

Also, being able to empathize with other people allows you to better deal with your emotions. It makes it a lot easier to treat yourself with care emotionally when you recognize that you are not the only one dealing with emotions that you carry. Despite our brain's propensity to exaggerate what we feel and make us feel like we are the only ones dealing with a certain situation or group of emotions, that is untrue. Being able to identify these emotions in other people allows you to see that you can overcome them when they become negative or seem like a force that is too much to bear.

Finding Balance

It is not enough to be emotionally intelligent in one part of your life and emotionally illiterate in another. There needs to be balance or the effects will spill into your entire life. It has been scientifically proven that there needs to be a balance of work and life for a person to be considered healthy and to perform their best in both areas. When one area suffers, so does the other.

While being more self-aware can help a person gain a better awareness of the things that need to change to be a well-balanced individual on all fronts, there needs to be active effort placed into attaining balance.

Regain Control of Your Life

Now, when it comes to regaining control of your life, you have a few options. You can work to protect yourself from dark psychology and manipulation just by working with yourself. Learning to set your boundaries and defend them is perhaps one of the greatest things that you can do that will allow you to regain control of your life and the sooner that you commit to doing so, the sooner that you can be free of the nonsense that will otherwise threaten to take over.

14. We are going to address first how to help yourself be protected. Then, we will consider how you can positively influence those around you.Defending Yourself From Manipulation Techniques

At this point in your reading, I assume you have a clear understanding of manipulation regarding what it is, how it happens, and its techniques. Maybe you are construing this book because you have been manipulated or feel you are being manipulated. When people realize they have been conducted, they may feel ashamed, weak, used, or stupid. Generally, being manipulated sucks, especially after learning that we have been unconsciously used to help people to further their selfish agendas.

Understand Your Rights

The main reason that you will feel as if someone is manipulating you is that you will feel as if your rights are violated. However, you would fail even to realize that somebody is operating you if you have no idea what fundamental rights you are entitled to. As long as you stick with your lane and don't harm people or interfere with their lives, you remain on the safe side. Fundamental rights are the appropriate boundaries that outline the extent to which one person can affect another's life. Therefore, one of the most effective ways to keep manipulators away is to know where your rights start and end. Below are a number of the common fundamental human rights:

- Everyone has the right to be accorded respect. If you realize that somebody is disrespecting you, it'd be a symbol of manipulation.

- Everyone has the right to work out their priorities. If you opt to prioritize yourself, nobody should attempt to interfere with that.

- Everyone has the free will to direct their wants, opinions, and feelings. As we have already seen, manipulation happens by taking away free will.

- Everyone has the right to refuse something without being made to feel guilty. This fact is often vital because if you realize that you don't want something, saying "no" should be respected.

- Everyone has the right to have opinions that differ from those of others. Disagreements are normal. Therefore, nobody should mistreat you in any way for holding different views.

Finally, and important to our topic of avoiding manipulation, everyone has the right to guard themselves against being emotionally, physically, or mentally threatened. Be free to object and walk away if you believe this right is being abused.

Hide Your Weaknesses

One way to enable it to happen is by allowing outsiders to understand our weaknesses. A manipulator's plan is typical to seek out their victim's weaknesses and use them to evoke the sensation of inadequacy, guilt, shame, blame, or weakness. Therefore, not unless it is indispensable, or the person you are opening up to has proven to be real and trustworthy, always keep your shortcomings hidden. The downside to opening up even to real friends is that you never know when the friendship might end.

To some extent, sharing our weaknesses isn't even necessary. Imperfections are part of being human, and there is a share of the same for all. Therefore, if you can keep the shortfalls to yourself and feel satisfied with them, it is often the best defense against manipulation. After all, everyone has their flaws, and they don't go around preaching about them. Once the manipulator has no shortcuts to accessing our most powerful emotions, they cannot succeed in invading our lives. In short, know what to share with others and what to keep only between you and yourself.

Call Them Out

A manipulator may have controlled people for a long time because nobody has ever confronted them. This fact is often an assumption, but it doesn't make the tactic any less significant. Manipulators are often bullying, too, and bullies are weak people that torture others who feel helpless before them. In short, don't let the manipulator feel you know they are using you but fear speaking it up. Allowing them to continue uninterrupted will only increase their power over you also because of the severity of their behavior. When it becomes clear that somebody is trying to mess with your mind, allow them to know that you are uncomfortable with it.

Calling out on the manipulator's behavior may have several positive effects. First, they will realize that you are awake enough to understand that they are trying mind tricks on you. Toxic people hate and are frightened of people with strong consciousness and self-esteem. Second, by calling them out, you would possibly be the first one that has ever stood up to them. The shock of being discovered plus the shame that comes with it is often a strong enough deterrent. If this is often the case, it will force them to understand the extent of their behavior. Assuming they are not chronic manipulators, they will change their ways.

Avoid Emotional Attachments

This approach is as easy to say than do, especially if you discover out too late that you are manipulated. It might even be hard to use if the manipulator is good at hiding their true colors initially. All the same, we must learn to detach our emotional connections with people that we feel are draining us. Well, there are red flags when a manipulator is close to entrapping you. One is that they are going to force premature feelings. For example, an individual you just met 2 days ago should sound suspicious if they begin saying how you'd make a perfect couple. It might be suicidal to swallow this bait and initiate an emotional attachment. Therefore, take longer before allowing new people to trap you with emotions.

In case you are already attached to a toxic person, you ought to work towards eliminating the bond. Realizing that somebody has been using you ought to be disappointing enough to melt the connection. Whenever your mind or heart attempts to welcome them back, remember what they have been doing to you. With time, you would have conditioned your mind to kick the emotional connection away. If you want to maintain the conversation, keep it civil, and move aside whenever they struggle to establish anything more than that.

Emotional connections are the manipulator's favorite tools. Destroy them!

Quit Harmful Relationships

Manipulators are often the people we are closest to, like family, spouses, friends, siblings, teachers, etc. This fact is usually sure to be scary, but it is the raw truth. Immediately you realize that anyone close to you is trying or has already manipulated you, you should cut the connection off. Many of us are afraid to give up due to their ties with them, but if you are conscious of the harm that manipulation can cause, you will not hesitate. If a girlfriend needs money or gifts reciprocally for love or sex, you should allow them to go. If a parent belittles you by comparing you to other people, you can rent a place to give them space and maintain respect.

Learn to Say No

You do not need to accept as right everything that is thrown at you. Remember that creating independent decisions is one of your fundamental rights. Your "no" doesn't need to be rude but diplomatic. By being diplomatic, I mean saying it and meaning it. People are keen on convincing others when they have already been told no. You need to make people understand that it is final and not up for debate when deciding. This fact is what we mean by setting yourself as a priority and commanding the respect that you deserve.

It is essential that once you say no, it shouldn't cause you to feel guilty. Sensible people understand that when an individual rejects something, it is not a personal reaction but a mere expression of freedom. Manipulators are stubborn people that do not like getting left. When handling them, make them know that you have made your decision and will not change your mind at all costs. If they persist, you will possibly get to apply a different technique intrinsically, our final method of avoiding manipulation: setting consequences.

Finding Inner Peace

Peace of mind is the ultimate goal for most people. It is so great to find that peaceful point—that point in which you are certain that you have done everything that you can and attempted to live the right life for yourself. That point in which you can accept that you are living your best life and enjoying it. Think of the lucky few who have achieved this—they are calm. They are patient. They can deal with just about anything with kindness. Despite just how easy these people make it seem; these people must work hard to make this sort of emotional state occur.

To be at peace is highly demanding on the mind, contrary to popular belief. To be at peace requires you to be able to develop enough emotional control to not give in whenever something goes wrong. To be at peace is to ensure that you can succeed accordingly. It is to recognize that ultimately, the ways that you behave in life are dependent upon your mindset.

If you want to be at peace, Stoicism is for you. Stoic philosophers have been pursuing that degree of peace for centuries. Marcus Aurelius dedicated every morning to working with his journals. Epictetus constantly stated that men are disturbed by the thoughts that are developed rather than what happens around them. People need to remember that ultimately, to be at peace is to be in control of the mind.

It is to be in control of the thoughts. Stoicism has endured for thousands of years and is still so popular because it allows for that degree of control that people want. It teaches people how they can begin to control themselves. It reminds them of what they need to do so that they can guide themselves throughout their lives on the right paths. If you can develop that ability to behave stoically, you can live a peaceful life.

Both Marcus Aurelius and Epictetus saw philosophy not as something to use now and then, but as a way of life—they constantly revisited the philosophies they were studying. They regarded the philosophy of stoicism as something that could be used to aid them in just about every aspect of life. They learned to become more reflective and less reactive. They turned inward instead of outward. They learned to keep their cool, to recognize that sometimes, the best thing that you can do in life is to simply let things go and move on.

When it comes right down to it, to be peaceful, to live your most successful, happiest life, you must embrace these concepts. You must let go of the impression that ultimately, you are stuck with your negativity or in the mindset that you are in. If you want to achieve inner peace yourself, there are steps that you can take to ensure that you make it happen. It may not be easy, but it is something that you can do for yourself. All you have to fix is set out to make it happen. We are going to look at the several steps toward finding inner peace as a Stoic. Live these ideas. Let them guide you and the life that you live. You will discover what matters the most in your life, and you will discover that you are all the happier for it.

15. SpeedReading to Understand People

Ultimately, being able to read other people is highly important. If you want to be able to understand what is going on in someone else's mind, you need to be able to tell what is going on with their bodies first. The truth is people are quite easy to learn to read if you know what you are doing. You just have to do is make sure that those clusters are being looked at by you.

Ultimately, we all communicate with people in different ways. We have both verbal and nonverbal signals that we give off at all times. However, the bulk of our communication is nonverbal. We have plenty of body language that we use in all sorts of different ways to be able to understand what is going on with other people. We look at things such as proximity to each other and general demeanor to figure out what is going on inside one person's mind so that we can get more information from them. When you do this, you learn to recognize how you can interpret what they are about to do, if they are going to do anything at all.

You will learn how to understand the basic expressions, attraction, closed behavior, assertiveness, and dominance. All of these are important in their ways, serving important roles that you can utilize. You just have to make sure you know what to look for!

Reading Expressions

Ultimately, we have 6 primary expressions—these are known as our universal expressions because you can spot them pretty much in any culture. No matter where you are from, you know what a smile is, and you can recognize it immediately. That is because a smile is an expression that is considered universal. Let's look at the 6 universal emotions now so that you can better see what to expect with them.

Happiness

Happiness is easy to understand. When you see someone that's happy, you can recognize it by the smile primarily. However, the most obvious sign of happiness is the crinkle in the eyes—this is how you know that the smile and happiness are legitimate.

Sadness

When it comes to sadness, you can identify it by the fact that the entire face melts, so to speak. You can see that the eyebrows go down. The corners of the mouth do as well, and the inner corners of the brows go up. There may or may not be crying involved as well.

Anger

Anger is defined by 3 primary characteristics, aside from the demeanor that goes with it. Usually, someone who is angry will have their brows lowered while pressing their lips together firmly. Alternatively, the mouth may be open, baring teeth, and squared.

Fear

Fear is usually shown as brows up high on the face, but still flat, with the eyes widened. The mouth also usually opens widely as well.

Surprise

Surprise is similar to fear in people, but the marked difference is that the jaw lowers alongside the opening of the mouth, and the eyes are usually opened wider, showing whites on both sides. The brows are also arched instead of just raised.

Disgust

Disgust is noticed primarily by taking a look at how the face comes together. The upper lip goes up, rising slightly. The nose bridge usually wrinkles as well, and the cheeks pinch in and up to try to protect the eyes.

Reading Attraction

When somebody is fascinated to someone else, they show very obvious body language as well. In particular, you can expect to see all sorts of specific actions. The body does not usually lie, and because of that, you can look directly at the behaviors that someone is doing to figure out if they are attracted to you or not. In particular, you want to look for the following behaviors:

Sustained Eye Contact

You will see that the other person will maintain eye contact more when they are attracted to you. Additionally, they will usually look away, and then glance right back to see if you're still watching them.

Smiling

There is a reason we assume smiling is flirting—it happens often. The flirty, attracted smile usually lasts longer and includes flirty eye contact as well, fleeting, but regular.

Self-Grooming

Men and women both do this—they brush their hair with their hands, adjust their clothes, and otherwise tamper with their appearance when they are flirting or talking to someone, they find attractive. If they do this regularly, they may be attracted to you.

Looking Nervous

Being nervous is a very normal thing when attracted to someone else, and this usually shows itself through fiddling with something repeatedly.

Leaning in

Typically, people will lean in toward things that they are attracted to, and people are no exception to that rule. You will also notice that the feet will point at the person that the individual is attracted to.

Licking the Lips

This is a common one, but it is subtle and easy to miss. However, you can notice it if you pay close attention. Usually, it is noticeable by a quick part of the lips and a small suck or lick.

Reading Assertiveness

Assertiveness is calm, confident, and in control. Effectively, if someone is assertive, they are behaving as if they are in control—they take charge, they are comfortable with themselves, but also won't go out of their way to overstep on other people either. They simply sit back and allow things to play out without letting anyone else dominate them. The most common signs of assertiveness include:

Smooth Body Movements

When you are assertive over something, you don't have jerky movements. They are smooth and in control without much of a problem, even when energized or emotional. The voice sounds smooth as well, and they slowly and steadily look about.

Balanced

The assertive individual is usually upright, relaxed, but also well balanced and comfortable.

Open Body Language

Usually, these people will show that they are open to engagement without being threatening or provocative. They do not block off their bodies at all and show open hands as well.

Eye-Contact Regularly

Eye contact is usually steady and maintained comfortably without much of a problem.

Smiling

There are plenty of polite smiles and listening well with this body language as well. Usually, you can expect the other person to be quite comfortable, and they will smile easily and appropriately.

Firm

While they are firm, they usually have a solid stance without much of a problem. They are not aggressive at all and usually show that they are willing to listen, but they are also firm. They do not escalate anything and tend to avoid aggression in any form.

Reading Domination

Domination is a little more than assertiveness. Usually, with assertiveness, you see someone that is showing that they are confident without being threatening. However, with dominance, you can expect to see a much more threatening demeanor. A dominating body is going to show signs such as:

Facial Aggressiveness

You will be able to see the aggression in the face—usually in the form of frowning and sneering or even snarling.

Starring

The aggressive individual will usually stare at someone that they don't like or may also squint or attempt to avoid looking at someone entirely.

Widebody Stance

They will usually stand out with their shoulders widened and may even hold their arms wide open as well. They may also stand with their hands placed firmly on their hips in a crotch display.

Sudden Movements

You may notice that the aggressor is very rough with his movements, moving about suddenly and even erratically sometimes. It is a good sign that he or she is not in a very good spot at that moment and may do something else aggressive as well.

Large Gestures

You may notice that as the individual moves, he will signal with aggressive, almost too big or wide movements that get close to you without ever getting close enough to touch you.

Reading Closed Behavior

Finally, let's go over closed behavior before we continue. Closed behavior shows that the individual is not interested in engaging with the other party at all. When you see closed behavior, you know that the individual is not going to want to engage with you; you know that you are going to see that they want to be left alone, or that they are not receptive to being interacted with then. You can expect to see signs of this sort of behavior, such as:

Crossed Arms

This is perhaps the most telltale sign. When someone is feeling closed off, they will almost always cross their arms and keep their hands near to their body. When they speak during this time, they will keep a monotone voice. Think of this as your sign that you are creating a barrier between yourself and the other party with your arms. You want to be left alone, so you close yourself off entirely.

Crossed Legs

You can also cross off legs as well—when you do this, you see that the knees are across from each other when sitting down, or they can also cross the ankles as well. This creates an even more closed-off image that shows that you are defensive and not willing to listen or change your viewpoint on something.

Looking Away

It is also very common to see that the closed-off person wants nothing to do with those around them. They don't want to look at the person that is engaging with them.

Leaning Away

You may also see that the closed-off person wants nothing to do with getting close to the individual that is engaging with them either. Instead, they will pull away and lean back, trying to put as much distance between them as possible.

Feet Turned Away

Look to the feet when you want to know how engaged someone else is. If you see that the other person is standing away, feet pointing away from you, they are closed off and don't want to engage in the conversation at all.

16. Finding Inner Peace

Sometimes we think that things are far worse than they may seem, and the unfortunate reality is that as soon as you do that, you find yourself in a constant spiral in which you want to do better, but you cannot. You get yourself stuck in this mindset of being unable to manage the current situation that you are in because you are too busy catastrophizing to realize that things are not that bad in the first place.

We tend to be more afraid of all of the what-ifs rather than the realities of situations, and because of that, it becomes important to let go of them. Yes, this is more laid-back said than done, but it is highly powerful. If you want to escape the anxiety that you have and live a Stoic life, you must be making it a point to engage with your life in the most beneficial way that you can muster. You must make sure that you work to provide yourself with everything that you know to be true. You must work to ensure that you can remind yourself that catastrophizing never helped anyone.

Remember Whose Opinions Matter the Most

Perhaps one of the largest sources of anxiety that we have these days comes from the worry about what other people think about us. We all constantly worry about what other people think about ourselves even though ultimately, we all tend to prioritize ourselves over other people. When it comes right down to it, the opinions of everyone around you are not as important as yours. When it comes right down to it, it is your opinion that matters the most, and when you recognize that and consider that, you can start to erase some of those worries that you have.

Think about it—today, we are endlessly connected online. We are constantly able to get back to people quickly and easily. We are all constantly inundated with opinions, and if it is on the internet, everyone has one. However, ultimately, when it comes right down to it, the only opinion that truly matters is yours. It does not matter what your neighbor thinks about your haircut—what do you think about it?

Humans are social animals, and because we are, we worry about what other people think about us. However, in reality, there are so many different people in the world with so many different opinions and desires that if you were to try to consider every single person's opinion, you would never get anything done. Why, then, do you let the people that are in your immediate vicinity pass judgment?

Keep your focus on what matters—your thoughts. Make sure that you live a life that makes you happy. Let go of the idea that you have to be liked by all. Instead, focus on what you can do to be kind and disciplined. What can you do to master tolerance over pain and displeasure? How can you maintain your patience? These are what matter. Ultimately, as soon as you stop caring about what everyone around you thinks, you will find that you are far happier than you thought that you would be.

Take Time to Be Still

If peace is what you want to achieve, then you have to live it as well. If you want to be truly peaceful, then you have to schedule the time to be at peace. Even in a rapidly evolving world, where we are constantly working on more and being busier than ever, you must take the time to ensure that you are calm and able to remind yourself that ultimately, the way that you behave matters more than anything else. If you want to be able to interact with people calmly, then you have to practice calmness.

Practicing peaceful stillness is a great way for you to embody what you want out of life. Remember, you must always practice what you preach, and this is where you start. If you want to be calm, then be physically calm. Take some time each day to spend time in peace, in stillness, and in quiet. This means that every single day, you need to prioritize some time in which you are doing nothing. No phones. No television. No talking to other people. You will sit quietly and enjoy the moment. This is all about making sure that you get to know the peace that you want.

This is difficult; however—we find that ultimately, people can't stop and reflect at the moment. You must be able to master this art—you must be able to remind yourself that ultimately, you need calmness in your life if you want to be successful in making sure that you are keeping up with your practice. The sooner that you can practice the calmness and stillness, the sooner that your mind will learn to reflect silently and peacefully.

Find the Beauty in Every Situation

Even though Stoicism pushes this idea that you ought to be unmoving, logical, and at peace, there is still enjoyment found within it. You should always take the time that you can find the beauty that exists. There is beauty in just about anything—you just have to know where or how to look. If you can do that, if you can figure out how to look at a situation and see the beauty in it, you can live the Stoic life with ease.

Think about it—even in a storm; there is something to look forward to. The grass and plants are getting much-needed water that they will use to provide for themselves. The animals will have new puddles that can be used to drink from. The water is pure and clean. There may be a rainbow. The sound of rain is refreshing and beautiful on its own. The smell of petrichor, that first moment in which rain starts to fall.

Beauty is visible everywhere around you. Beauty can be found in even the darkest of places, and when you realize that even those things in the world that could be painful or difficult to deal with can have some beauty in them, even if that beauty is not yet apparent to you at the moment, it can become apparent to you in the future. You can learn what it is that matters. You can learn to recognize that beauty and respect it. You can discover what it will take for you to accept what has happened so that you can respond accordingly.

The next time that you are walking somewhere stops and considers the beauty of the blue sky. Enjoy the taste of the coffee that you are sipping instead of chugging it down to get that caffeine before rushing off. Stop and savor the feeling of hot water running down your back in the shower. It will be worth it.

Imagine a New Perspective

It is so easy to get trapped up in the moment when something is going wrong. It is so easy to find that you are constantly worrying about the moment that you suddenly are missing something. You can get stuck in what you see in front of you—but really, what if you consider a different perspective? What if you imagined yourself from above the problem instead of beside it?

Think about it—imagine that your car just died. You are frustrated. However, if you were to stop and imagine it from a bird's perspective, the car would probably not even be a blip on its radar. You can move further up—from an airplane; you could not even see your broken-down car. Even higher, you may not be able to see your street or even your city.

The universe is immense. When you are feeling that emotions are running high, you can remind yourself of the insignificance of the moment. Why get so worked up over something that is not that big after all? If you want to be in a mindset of peace, this is not how you achieve it. If you are not careful, you will find that you are not able to maintain that peace at all—you are going to be stuck in the negativity of the situation. The next time that you feel that you are upset try reimagining the situation. If you were to look at things from the top down, how significant would it be?

Follow Your Code

Stoicism creates a framework that we can live by—it is a list of guidelines that we can use to reflect upon the world and determine how we align ourselves with it. If you look at the way that you engage with the world through the lens of code, you remind yourself that ultimately, you have set behaviors that you want to follow. The code becomes a sort of way for you to determine what is good and what is bad.

This helps you to achieve that inner peace as a Stoic for one reason: it simplifies things. When you approach the situation as a Stoic, you know that you are working to avoid letting emotionality play a role in your decisions. You are looking at things as rationally and logically as you can because you hope that in doing so, you can make sure that you make the right choices. Rationality becomes your code, and that brings you peace. When you know your place and what is expected of you, it is easy to be in that position or state of peace, and you will not have to do much more to maintain it. Simply make sure that you are following your code and not violating it. If it is wrong, do not do it. Stand by your convictions. Follow your moral code of conduct. If you can do this, you will be at peace with yourself.

Reflect

Finally, if you wish to achieve inner peace, the most important of all is to reflect. Make sure that you reflect upon your days every single day. In particular, Stoics tend to prefer the art of journaling. It works well to allow you to gather your thoughts, to address why you did what you did. It allows you to think about how you can better yourself in the future, or what you can do if you want to change the interactions that you have with those in your area. Though you can ultimately reflect in any way that you want to, to reflect through journaling gives you a wonderful way through which you can make sure that you are documenting all of the details. This will ensure that you know that you did something a certain way and what the implications are.

To reflect is to observe. To reflect on what matters the most in your life, you can focus where it matters—on the ways that you should be interacting with people. On how you can stay true to yourself. You can reason with yourself so that you can continue to better yourself. Every single day, you will become more and more aware of yourself and your habits, and through becoming more aware, you will find that ultimately, you have made some major moves toward being the successful Stoic that you want to be. Remember, you are always a work in progress, and through journaling, you will bring yourself closer to that feeling of peace.

Conclusion

D ark psychology is the art of mind control and manipulation.

Manipulation may be defined as a process by which one person (manipulator) induces another person to behave in a manner that is desired by the manipulator but not by the other person.Manipulation is done through a complex process of implementing thoughts and actions in such a way that they result in the behavior of the target individual (manipulated person) being similar to what the manipulator desires.In the course of advancing toward their goal, the manipulator may use several tactics including emotional manipulation, physical manipulation, and verbal manipulation among others.

The ways to avoid this complex phenomenon are difficult to articulate because there are several levels on which people can be manipulated.For instance, there are specific ways to avoid becoming a victim of physical manipulation.For instance, don't accept food or drink from strangers.If you must accept any food or drink from anybody, make sure the person is somebody you know and trust for a long time.

There are also specific ways to avoid being a victim of manipulation by way of verbal means.One should never share personal information with people you don't trust completely.You should always ask permission from the person with whom you share your personal information.This will help you remain in control of your privacy as much as possible.

There are several ways in which people can be emotionally manipulated and there are some steps that can help them avoid it. Don't allow yourself to get caught up in other people's anger, pain, or sorrow.You may be empathetic but do not allow yourself to be manipulated and controlled by other people's emotions.